GROUNDED

LEADERSHIP

HOW TO LEAD WITH INFLUENCE BEYOND TITLES

Richard Englander

Foreword

I have spent much of my life studying leadership, reading about it, teaching it, and, most importantly, living it with my assistant coaches who find themselves in the unheralded middle. Titles come and go, but the quiet, steady influence of those who lead without fanfare is what keeps teams alive, organizations moving, and student-athletes growing. That is why "Grounded Leadership: How to Lead with Influence Beyond Titles" landed on my desk at exactly the right moment.

Richard Englander does not write from the mountaintop. He writes from the middle, the place where vision collides with reality, the reality of motivating young people to strive for excellence through challenging and difficult environments. I have stood there as the leader trying to rally a skeptical team, as a parent guiding children through uncertainty, and as a leader of a volunteer organization trying to achieve a goal for the team without personal gain. In every case, the question was the same: "How do I move people forward when I am not the one who set the vision, but I am responsible for helping achieve it?"

As a Head of Schools (CEO) and as a head football coach who oversees 120 employees, this book gives clarity of leadership with a rare blend of practicality. It provides tools to keep our organization moving forward.

Richard's insights as a business owner, coach, teacher, and father give him unique experiences to provide solutions for the leader in the middle and to keep us moving forward. The book provides a unified portrait of leadership as service, discipline, and love, and influence as stewardship. These are not only anecdotes designed to impress but honest reflections that invite us to see our own struggles through his eyes.

What sets this work apart is its refusal to separate skill from soul. Too many leadership books offer frameworks without formation, tactics without transformation. Richard insists that you cannot lead others until you have led yourself, and you cannot lead yourself without anchoring your identity in something larger than ambition. He turns to Scripture not as decoration but as infrastructure, showing how ancient wisdom speaks directly to modern dilemmas, whether you are managing a classroom, a small business, or a team.

As I read, I found myself nodding at familiar tensions: the frustration of having insight without authority, the loneliness of carrying out decisions that affect lives while receiving little credit, the quiet joy of watching someone else succeed because you stayed steady when no one was watching. Richard names these moments without sentimentality and equips us to navigate them with purpose. This is not a book for those waiting for permission to lead. It is for those already leading, often without realizing it, and hungry for language, tools, and encouragement to do it better. If you have ever felt overlooked yet indispensable, stretched yet called, this book will feel like a conversation with a mentor who has walked your road and refuses to let you walk it alone.

J.T. Curtis

Head of John Curtis Christian School

Head Football Coach

Dedication

To my wife, *Tammy*, whose steadfast love, faith, and wisdom have been a constant source of strength and encouragement. You embody the truth that "two are better than one, because they have a good reward for their labor" (Ecclesiastes 4:9). Your grace and covenant have enriched every step of this journey.

To my children, Zach, Tim, Josh, Jonny, and Harvest, whose lives remind me daily of God's promises and purpose. "Children are a heritage from the Lord, the fruit of the womb a reward" (Psalm 127:3). May you continue to walk with integrity, courage, and faith as you fulfill your God-given callings.

To my son, Josiah, even though I have never held you physically in my arms, you are in my heart daily, and I look forward to the day I can see you face to face.

To my mentor, *Coach J.T. Curtis*, whose example of discipline, humility, and unwavering faith has profoundly shaped my understanding of leadership. As Scripture teaches, "Give honor to whom honor is due" (Romans 13:7). Your guidance and example have been a lasting investment in my life and calling.

This book is dedicated with deep gratitude to each of you—for your influence, your faith, and the legacy of excellence you continue to inspire.

Acknowledgement

I would like to express my deepest appreciation to my **wife** and *family* for their endless love, patience, and encouragement throughout this journey. Your faith in me has been my greatest support system.

A significant thank you to my former managers for the guidance and inspiration that helped shape many of the lessons displayed in this book.

To my dad, ***Richard Englander Jr.,*** Words cannot express how grateful I am for your wisdom and support every step of the way. A book would be as much yours as it is mine.

And lastly, my deepest appreciation to the team of ***Visionary Publishers Co.*** for their commitment, creativity, and faith in this project. Your collaboration made this vision a reality.

About The Author

Richard Englander is a practitioner of leadership in the spaces where vision meets daily reality. A former business owner, high school teacher, department head, championship-winning coach, and ministry leader, he has spent more than two decades guiding teams, students, athletes, and communities through growth, crisis, and change, rarely from the top of the chart, almost always from the vital middle.

In business, he doubled revenue in a small fitness enterprise while learning the weight of decisions that affect livelihoods. On the sidelines, he coached teams to state titles, discovering that discipline and encouragement build more than wins. In classrooms and accreditation seasons, he led faculty and students toward excellence, proving that influence often outpaces authority. In ministry, he has helped plant and shepherd communities rooted in faith and purpose.

Richard holds a master's degree in education and has trained leaders across sectors in communication, team development, and resilient decision-making. He writes and speaks from experience, not theory, blending practical frameworks with Scriptural wisdom to equip everyday leaders who carry responsibility without always holding the final say.

He lives with his family in Louisiana, where he continues to lead, learn, and lift others up, one conversation, one team, one season at a time.

Table of Contents

Introduction

Imagine standing in the middle of a busy intersection, not at the start of the road, not at the destination, but right where paths cross and decisions happen. This is where most leadership lives.

It's not in the corner office with the big title or the applause of the crowd; it's in the spaces between vision and execution, between strategy and reality, where influence must be earned, not commanded.

It's in these moments that leaders shape outcomes, inspire people, and hold organizations together, not through authority alone, but through clarity, courage, and the quiet power of example.

Leadership in the middle is challenging. It requires navigating competing priorities, motivating teams without always having the final word, and making an impact when recognition may be scarce. Yet, it is here, often unseen, often underappreciated, that the heartbeat of every successful organization truly beats.

This book is an invitation to step into that space, to recognize the power you already possess, and to learn how to lead with purpose, faith, and influence, regardless of your current position.

Leadership is everywhere in today's world. From corporate boardrooms to classrooms, from sports fields to community organizations, everyone is looking for leaders who bring clarity, direction, and strength.

Yet, too often, leadership is measured by title, by who sits at the top, who has the corner office, or who calls the shots.

The reality is that true leadership rarely lives at the very top. It thrives in the middle. It lives in the space between vision and execution, between strategy and day-to-day reality, between those giving direction and those carrying it out. This is where leaders wrestle with competing priorities, navigate limited authority, and still manage to inspire growth. The middle is the glue that holds organizations together.

I know this firsthand because my own journey has been about leading from the middle. I've led as a business owner striving to keep a small company thriving. I've led as a coach, standing shoulder to shoulder with young athletes, teaching them discipline and teamwork. I've led as a teacher and department head, guiding students and colleagues toward personal and professional growth. I've led in ministry, helping build communities of faith and purpose. In each season, I wasn't always the one with the final say, but I was always someone with responsibility, influence, and opportunity.

This book invites you to view leadership in a new light. Leadership is not about waiting until you're in charge to make a difference. It's about recognizing the influence you already have, no matter where you stand on the organizational chart. The middle is not a place of limitation; it is a place of power.

How This Book Is Different

You may have noticed that many books today carry the title *Leading from the Middle*. What makes this one different isn't just the words on the cover, it's the heartbeat behind them.

This book isn't written only for executives in glass towers or managers with corner offices. It's for anyone who has responsibility, influence, and the desire to make a real difference, whether in a business, a school, a team, a ministry, or even a family.

I've led across many arenas, and each has shaped me in ways I could never have predicted. In business, I have learned that the weight of decisions that affect livelihoods is significant, and the joy of seeing a team thrive is invaluable. As a coach, I experienced the power of encouragement, discipline, and teamwork firsthand. In education, I guided students and colleagues toward growth, learning that influence often matters more than authority. In ministry, I have seen how servant leadership fosters community and transforms lives. These experiences taught me that leadership principles are universal, but the way we live them out depends on the context and the people around us.

What makes this book perfect for everyone is that it doesn't just talk about leadership in theory. It blends real-world experience with timeless wisdom. The pages that follow draw on Scripture to show how the lessons Jesus taught about serving others are just as relevant today, whether you are leading a team at work, a classroom of students, or a group in your community.

I also wrote this book with complete honesty. Leadership is not a straight path. There are detours, setbacks, and moments of doubt. This book doesn't shy away from those realities; it leans into them, because the challenges are what teach us resilience, empathy, and vision.

Also, beyond strategy, this book is about identity. Leadership is not just a set of skills; it's a reflection of who you are called to be. The tools, principles, and stories here are meant to help you lead with character, faith, and vision. I hope you don't just gain ideas to implement, but also create a deeper sense of purpose, confidence, and a clear calling.

At the end of the day, leadership is more about the impact you make rather than the status you hold. That is the true power of leading from the middle.

I remember sitting in a conference room, watching executives discuss plans that would affect dozens of people. My team looked to me for guidance, but I didn't have the final say. I was "*in the middle,*" a place that often feels invisible, overlooked, and transparent, which was a little frustrating. And yet, in that moment, I realized something important: *influence doesn't come from a title. It comes from the choices we make, the trust we build, and the example we set.*

That's the heart of this book. This isn't a memoir, though you'll hear stories from my journey. It isn't a textbook or a dense academic treatise. And it isn't a sermon or devotional, though Scripture will weave through these pages as a source of guidance and wisdom. **What is this book then?** It is a companion, practical, faith-informed, and human, for those who find themselves leading from the middle.

If you've ever felt the tension of responsibility without authority, you're not alone. You may be a manager, a team lead, a volunteer coordinator, or someone carrying influence quietly behind the scenes.

You know what it's like to have ideas, insight, and vision, and to wonder if anyone will actually listen. You are also aware of the satisfaction that comes from seeing your efforts ripple outward, shaping culture, driving projects, and empowering others.

This book is for you. It's for the leader who wants to make a difference without stepping on anyone. It's for the person who wants to carry vision, inspire trust, and grow in character while guiding others. Most of all, it's for those who understand that authentic leadership isn't about a title or position, it's about influence, service, and the impact you leave behind.

Through the following chapters, we'll explore what it means to lead from the middle: how to influence without authority, communicate effectively, develop people, and lead yourself first.

We'll combine practical frameworks, real-life examples, reflection exercises, and Scriptural insights to help you navigate the challenges and seize the opportunities of your position.

Because here's the truth: no matter where you are on the organizational chart, you can make a difference. You can lead well, and you can influence beyond your authority. And in doing so, you're stepping into the kind of leadership that matters most, leadership that shapes people, teams, and even organizations from the inside out.

Prologue

Most people imagine leadership as standing at the very top, in a corner office, a championship podium, or as the person with ultimate authority. The CEO, entrepreneur, head coach, and manager must be honored for their position; however, impactful leadership rarely lives in titles or positions.

It is the leadership in the trenches that carries influence, vision, and the courage to serve others wherever you are planted.

I've walked this path across many arenas: business, education, athletics, and ministry. I've stood on the sidelines of state championship games, led classrooms buzzing with curiosity, managed the growth of a small business, and guided communities searching for direction. Each setting looked different, but the mission remained the same: *to build people, cultivate trust, and create spaces where others could thrive.*

From doubling revenue in a fitness business to helping a school grow during critical seasons, from guiding teachers through accreditation to coaching athletes toward victory, I've learned one thing over and over: leadership isn't about being in charge, it's about taking responsibility, setting the tone, and inspiring growth.

The victories that last aren't measured on scoreboards or spreadsheets; they're seen in lives transformed through encouragement, discipline, and faith.

This book is for those who may feel "in the middle," not at the top, not holding the loudest microphone, but still carrying influence that matters. The middle is where vision meets reality, where challenges become opportunities, and where ordinary people step up to do extraordinary work.

As you turn these pages, my hope is that you'll see both the lessons I've learned and the possibilities waiting for you.

It is essential to remember that leadership isn't reserved for a select few; it's a calling for anyone willing to invest in others, persevere through challenges, and lead with purpose.

Jesus reminded us of this when He said,

"Whoever wants to become great among you must be your servant."

— (Matthew 20:26)

True greatness isn't about climbing higher; it's about lifting others up.

This is the story of leading from the middle, and the transformative power it has to change lives, organizations, and communities.

"Leadership is not about a title or a designation. It's about impact, influence, and inspiration."

— Robin S. Sharma

"Each of you should use whatever gift you have received to serve others, as faithful stewards of God's grace in its various forms."

— 1 Peter 4:10

Chapter 1:
The Power of Middle Leadership

Introduction

When most people think of leadership, they picture a top-down hierarchy: executives at the helm giving orders, and employees following instructions. However, in reality, the actual engine of most organizations rarely sits at the very top; it runs through the middle. Middle leaders are the bridge, the glue, and often the unsung heroes who drive culture, productivity, and innovation every day.

Middle leadership occupies a uniquely powerful position, as it connects the vision of senior management with the realities of the front lines. Executives may set strategy, but it is the middle leader who translates that strategy into actionable plans, ensuring high-level goals become tangible tasks that teams can implement effectively. In this way, middle leaders are translators, communicators, and implementers all at once; they turn vision into results.

I've witnessed this firsthand in every arena I've worked in. In education, as a department head, curriculum changes stalled until a middle leader coached the teacher, clarified expectations, and developed actionable steps that brought the vision to life. In business, strategic growth plans often looked perfect on paper, but only when middle managers worked closely with frontline staff, addressed concerns, and smoothed processes did we see revenue double. Even on the sports field, assistant coaches often translate the head coach's strategy into drills and exercises that players can execute, turning a plan into victory.

The Strategic Vantage Point of Middle Leadership

Middle leaders occupy a unique vantage point. It is positioned between the strategic vision of executives and the operational realities of frontline teams. This dual perspective allows them to see both the big picture and the granular details from the bird's-eye view, which makes them indispensable catalysts for organizational success.

A **2023** Gallup study highlights that middle managers drive **70%** of employee engagement, directly influencing retention, morale, and productivity. Their proximity to teams enables them to identify issues, such as declining motivation or process inefficiencies, while their access to leadership ensures alignment with broader goals.

For example, imagine a hospital unit manager tasked with implementing a new patient care protocol mandated by the board. The executive instruction is clear, but it is the unit manager who trains nurses, adjusts schedules, and handles resistance, ultimately improving patient outcomes by 15%.

Similarly, in a tech startup, a product manager takes a CEO's vision for a new feature and breaks it into development sprints, ensuring the team delivers on time. This strategic position empowers middle leaders to bridge aspiration and action, turning abstract goals into measurable results.

The Role and Influence of Middle Leaders

Middle leaders wield significant influence, often without formal authority. They are closest to staff; they are the ones who notice when morale dips, when a team member struggles, or when motivation wanes.

A well-supported team thrives; a disconnected one falters. In ministry, I have seen volunteers disengage when they didn't feel supported, or even when the pastor's vision was clear. A caring middle leader who invests time, listens actively, and encourages others can transform the participation, energy, and commitment of the executive employees.

Middle leaders are also frontline problem-solvers. They anticipate challenges, address issues promptly, and make decisions that prevent minor obstacles from escalating into major crises. They guide teams through change and help people navigate transitions while keeping operations running smoothly. Their role as change agents is critical; organizations depend on middle leaders to turn abstract goals into practical results.

Perhaps most importantly, middle leaders shape the future. They mentor and empower junior staff, cultivate new talent, and develop the next generation of leaders.

Through these efforts, they create a multiplier effect: amplifying senior leadership's vision while increasing team productivity, engagement, and confidence. On sports teams, for example, assistant coaches often develop future head coaches by modeling leadership, teaching techniques, and instilling discipline, ensuring a legacy of leadership continues.

A biblical example of middle leadership is Joseph in Egypt (*Genesis 41*).

Though not the Pharaoh, Joseph was entrusted with enormous responsibility. He translated Pharaoh's vision into practical action by organizing the storage of grain during years of plenty to prepare for famine. His foresight, planning, and execution saved countless lives. Joseph's story illustrates how middle leaders act as bridges between vision and execution, using wisdom, influence, and decisive action to create lasting impact.

Expanded Roles: The Multifaceted Middle Leader

Beyond the core responsibilities outlined, middle leaders take on additional roles that amplify their influence:

- **Conflict Mediators:** Middle leaders resolve disputes that could derail the progress of important tasks. At a nonprofit, a program coordinator mediated between volunteers and board members over event priorities, ensuring a fundraising campaign raised **20%** more than projected. This role requires diplomacy and emotional intelligence.

- **Resource Optimizers:** They maximize limited resources. A retail manager reallocated staff schedules to cover peak hours, boosting sales by **10%** without additional hiring.

- **Feedback Catalysts:** Middle leaders provide critical insights to executives. A logistics supervisor's feedback on driver challenges led to a revised delivery protocol, reducing errors by **12%**.

- **Culture Architects:** They shape team values. A school administrator's emphasis on collaboration fostered a culture of trust, improving teacher retention by **15%**.
- **Innovation Drivers:** They propose creative solutions. A manufacturing team lead introduced a quality control app, cutting defects by **8%**.

These roles highlight the versatility of middle leaders, who balance multiple responsibilities to drive organizational success.

Biblical Wisdom: Esther's Influence

Scripture offers another powerful example of middle leadership in Esther (*Esther 4–7*).

As a queen, Esther lacked ultimate authority but used strategic communication and courage to influence King Xerxes, saving her people from destruction. Her ability to navigate a complex political environment with wisdom and faith mirrors the challenges middle leaders face today. Esther's story challenges us to lead with integrity, leveraging influence to achieve transformative outcomes within constraints.

Roles and Responsibilities

Middle leaders carry several critical responsibilities that help the organization sustain success:

Translating Strategic Goals into Actionable Plans

Middle leaders take high-level directives and break them into practical steps that teams can implement without facing any difficulties.

For example, when a department manager receives a company-wide initiative to improve customer satisfaction, they create a step-by-step plan for the customer service team, including training, feedback processes, and weekly performance tracking, turning strategy into action.

Motivating and Developing Team Members

Middle leaders provide coaching, mentorship, and feedback to help individuals grow professionally while making sure that efforts align with organizational goals. A team leader who meets regularly with employees to discuss goals, offer guidance, and celebrate achievements fosters engagement, loyalty, and professional development.

Facilitating Communication Between Leadership Levels

Middle leaders serve as the communication bridge between executives and staff. A project manager, for instance, compiles progress reports for leadership while clarifying expectations and objectives for the team, ensuring alignment across levels.

Identifying Opportunities for Improvement and Innovation

Being close to day-to-day operations allows middle leaders to spot inefficiencies and propose process improvements. A shift supervisor noticing bottlenecks in production might implement a new workflow that reduces errors and accelerates output.

Maintaining Accountability for Outcomes

Middle leaders ensure teams meet objectives and deliver quality results, tracking performance, addressing issues proactively, and holding both themselves and their teams accountable. A sales manager who sets clear targets, monitors progress, and takes corrective action exemplifies this responsibility.

The Multiplier Effect of Middle Leadership

Middle leaders create a multiplier effect, amplifying impact across organizations. By mentoring, they develop future leaders, as seen when a marketing team lead coached an intern into a full-time role, strengthening team capacity.

By solving problems, they enhance efficiency, like a hospital unit manager who streamlined patient intake, reducing wait times by **25%**. By fostering trust, they build resilient cultures, as a community organizer did by creating feedback channels, boosting engagement.

A **2024** Harvard Business Review study found that middle leaders who excel at influence increase team productivity by **22%** and organizational agility by **18%**. Their dual perspective, understanding both strategy and operations, makes them uniquely positioned to align efforts, resolve conflicts, and drive innovation. This multiplier effect turns small actions into organization-wide impact.

Challenges and Opportunities

Middle leaders often encounter different and multiple challenges at the same time. However, each challenge presents opportunities for growth and influence:

Balancing Competing Priorities

They must navigate organizational goals while meeting team needs. For instance, a nurse manager might balance efficiency metrics set by administrators with the need to provide compassionate patient care. Tools such as Eisenhower's Urgent-Important Matrix or agile project management techniques help leaders make wise decisions.

The Bible reminds us of the importance of delegation and prioritization: Moses, advised by Jethro (*Exodus 18*), empowered capable leaders to handle responsibilities, freeing him to focus on the most critical tasks.

Leading Without Full Authority

Middle leaders often guide teams without full control over resources or policies. Success entirely depends on influence rather than command. Emotional intelligence, empathy, and integrity are essential tools for achieving success.

Nehemiah, who led the rebuilding of Jerusalem's walls (*Nehemiah 2:17*), demonstrates this principle: he inspired people to action not by authority, but through vision, encouragement, and s

trategic delegation.

Navigating Organizational Politics

Every organization has structures of influence and competing interests. Middle leaders must interpret directives from above, advocate for their teams, and maintain relationships with peers.

Daniel in Babylon provides a biblical model: he maintained integrity, built trust, and executed his duties effectively within a complex political system. Middle leaders today can emulate this by approaching organizational politics with transparency, fairness, and relational influence.

Practical Tips for Effective Middle Leadership

- **Communicate Clearly and Frequently:** Keep teams informed about goals, expectations, and updates.

- **Develop Emotional Intelligence:** Understand the motivations and concerns of team members and executives.

- **Prioritize Strategically:** Employ tools to balance urgent versus important tasks.

- **Empower Teams:** Delegate responsibilities and encourage initiative.

- **Build Relationships Across Levels:** Foster trust with peers, staff, and senior leaders.

- **Seek Feedback and Reflect:** Use input to grow personally and improve team effectiveness.

Expanded Practical Strategies

To further equip middle leaders, consider these additional strategies, each paired with a fresh example:

- **Leverage Storytelling:** Share relatable stories to align teams with goals. A restaurant manager used customer success stories to inspire staff, reducing complaints by **12%**.

- **Foster Psychological Safety:** Create environments where teams feel safe to share ideas. A tech team lead encouraged open feedback, leading to a **15%** increase in innovative proposals.

- **Use Data-Driven Insights:** Analyze metrics to guide decisions. A retail supervisor tracked sales patterns to optimize staffing, boosting revenue by **10%**.

- **Model Resilience:** Demonstrate adaptability during setbacks. A nonprofit coordinator maintained team morale during funding cuts, securing a new grant through persistence.

- **Invest in Cross-Training:** Develop versatile teams. A manufacturing lead cross-trained workers, improving production flexibility by **20%**.

These strategies are grounded in real-world success and enhance middle leaders' ability to navigate complex roles.

Real-Life Examples

Individuals, during their time at Google, influenced product strategy and team culture without being the top executive, showing how middle leaders drive results and cohesion. In ministry, a volunteer leader transformed youth engagement by organizing programs and mentoring others. In education, a teacher leader implemented mentoring for new staff, improving retention and performance. These examples demonstrate that leadership is less about titles and more about actions, influence, and culture.

Consider a logistics manager at a global retailer who streamlined supply chain processes by collaborating with warehouse staff and executives, reducing delivery times by **15%**. Or a community health coordinator who turned a vague directive to "improve outreach" into a targeted campaign, increasing participation by **20%**. These stories highlight how middle leaders translate vision into action, often without formal authority.

Global Perspectives on Middle Leadership

Middle leadership varies across cultural contexts. In collectivist cultures like Japan, middle leaders emphasize consensus, as seen when a factory manager facilitated group discussions to implement a new process, gaining buy-in and improving efficiency by **10%**.

In individualist cultures like the U.S., they focus on direct communication, like a startup manager pitching ideas to executives, securing funding for a new project.

A case study from Brazil shows a middle manager in a tech firm bridging developers and executives through collaborative workshops, aligning teams for a product launch that increased market share by **12%**.

Understanding cultural nuances enhances influence, whether building relationships in high-context cultures or driving results in low-context ones.

Practical Tool: The Influence Blueprint

To apply these insights, try this "Influence Blueprint" exercise:

- **Map Stakeholders:** List five people or groups you influence (e.g., team, peers, executives).

- **Assess Current Impact:** Note one way you currently influence each (e.g., mentoring, problem-solving).

- **Identify Growth Areas:** Choose one stakeholder and brainstorm a new way to expand your influence (e.g., proposing a process improvement).

- **Plan and Act:** Develop a one-week action plan to implement your idea and journal the outcome.

This exercise helps you visualize and grow your influence, grounding the chapter's lessons in your context.

The Lasting Legacy of Middle Leadership

Middle leaders leave a lasting legacy by shaping people, processes, and culture. A teacher leader who mentors new staff improves school performance for years.

A team lead who streamlines operations boosts long-term efficiency. A volunteer coordinator who builds trust strengthens community impact. These actions, though often unseen, create enduring change.

Scripture reinforces this in 1 Peter 4:10:

"As each has received a gift, use it to serve one another, as good stewards of God's varied grace."

Middle leadership is a calling to serve, to bridge, and to build, leaving a legacy that transcends titles.

Weekly Plan of Action: Building Your Influence

To apply the principles of middle leadership, follow this seven-day plan to amplify your influence, communication, and team engagement. Each day focuses on a specific action and is designed to be practical and measurable.

Day 1: Assess Your Influence

- **Action:** Identify three stakeholders you influence (e.g., team members, peers, executives) and note one way you currently impact each (e.g., mentoring, problem-solving).
- **Goal:** Gain clarity on your current influence.
- **Reflection:** Journal how your actions align with organizational goals. What strengths can you leverage?

Day 2: Clarify Communication

- **Action:** Hold a brief team meeting or send a clear, concise update on a current goal or project, emphasizing its "why."
- **Goal:** Ensure team alignment and understanding.
- **Reflection:** Did your message resonate? How can you improve clarity?

Day 3: Build Emotional Intelligence

- **Action:** Have a one-on-one conversation with a team member to understand their motivations or challenges. Listen actively without interrupting.
- **Goal:** Strengthen trust and empathy.
- **Reflection:** What did you learn about their perspective? How can you support them?

Day 4: Prioritize Strategically

- **Action:** Use Eisenhower's Urgent-Important Matrix to prioritize your tasks for the week. Delegate one non-critical task to a team member.

- **Goal:** Focus on high-impact responsibilities.
- **Reflection:** Did delegation free up time? How did it empower your team?

Day 5: Foster Innovation

- **Action:** Identify one process or workflow in your team that could be improved. Propose a small, actionable change (e.g., a new tool or streamlined step).
- **Goal:** Drive incremental improvement.
- **Reflection:** What was the initial response to your idea? How can you refine it?

Day 6: Strengthen Relationships

- **Action:** Connect with a peer or senior leader to discuss a shared goal or challenge. Offer a specific idea or insight.
- **Goal:** Build cross-level trust.
- **Reflection:** Did the interaction strengthen collaboration? What follow-up is needed?

Day 7: Reflect and Plan

- **Action:** Review the week's actions and outcomes. Journal one key lesson and set a goal for the next week to expand your influence.
- **Goal:** Consolidate learning and plan for growth.
- **Reflection:** How did this week's actions enhance your leadership? What's your next step?

This plan empowers you to apply middle leadership principles systematically. This strategic plan helps you to build skills and impact over time.

Reflection Questions

1. Which middle leadership role (e.g., translator, motivator) resonates most with your experience?
2. How can you expand your influence within your current position?

3. What challenge (e.g., balancing priorities, navigating politics) feels most pressing, and how can you address it?

Conclusion

Middle leadership is often overlooked, yet it is essential for organizational success. Middle leaders are the bridge between vision and execution, serving as influencers who engage and motivate employees, and as problem-solvers who keep operations running smoothly.

Though the role comes with challenges, balancing priorities, leading without full authority, and navigating politics, it also offers unparalleled opportunities for growth, influence, and long-term impact.

By mastering their responsibilities and leveraging influence, middle leaders become the linchpins of their organizations, turning strategy into results, inspiring teams, and shaping the future.

"The task of leadership is not to put greatness into people, but to elicit it, for the greatness is there already."

— John Buchan.

"As each has received a gift, use it to serve one another, as good stewards of God's varied grace."

— 1 Peter 4:10

Chapter 2:
The Unique Challenges of the Middle

In Chapter 1, we explored the profound power of middle leadership and his/her ability to bridge vision and execution, inspire teams, and shape organizational success through influence rather than authority.

Middle leaders are the linchpins who translate strategies into results, foster growth, and build trust across levels. Yet, this pivotal role comes with unique challenges that test resilience, adaptability, and wisdom. From balancing competing priorities to navigating organizational politics, middle leaders operate in a dynamic space where demands from above and below converge.

This chapter delves into these challenges, offering practical strategies, real-world examples, and biblical insights to equip you to thrive in the middle, transforming obstacles into opportunities for growth and impact.

Introduction

Middle leadership is a position of influence, responsibility, and constant challenge. Unlike top executives, middle leaders often carry the weight of executing strategic goals while guiding teams, frequently without full authority.

They operate in a space where vision meets reality, where expectations from above meet the needs of those on the frontlines. In my twenty years of experience across education, athletics, and business, I have faced these challenges firsthand. The lessons I have learned are deeply tied to stories, moments of struggle, and victories that shaped my understanding of what it means to lead from the middle.

This chapter delves into the unique challenges of middle leadership, illustrating each through real-life examples and practical strategies, framed by biblical wisdom.

The Complex Landscape of Middle Leadership

Middle leaders navigate a complex landscape, balancing competing demands, limited authority, and the pressure to deliver results. Their role requires them to be agile, empathetic, and strategic, often under intense scrutiny from both above and below.

A **2024** Deloitte study found that middle managers report **30%** higher stress levels than senior executives due to their dual responsibilities, yet their contributions drive **65%** of organizational agility. This tension defines middle leadership, making it both demanding and transformative.

Consider a project manager at a tech firm tasked with delivering a new software feature. Executives demand rapid deployment, while developers face technical constraints.

The manager must understand both sides, manage expectations, and ensure progress, all without full control over resources. This scenario, repeated across industries, underscores the unique challenges middle leaders face and the resilience required to thrive.

1. Balancing Competing Priorities

One of the first lessons I learned as a Social Studies Department Head was the delicate art of balancing priorities. My responsibilities spanned guiding new teachers through accreditation, improving academic performance, tracking student growth, and juggling administrative deadlines. On any given day, I moved between classroom teaching, curriculum planning, staff meetings, and extracurricular coaching.

It often felt like juggling flaming torches while walking a tightrope. One week, I finalized curriculum maps while coaching football after school; the next, I prepared students for mid-term exams while conducting department meetings. To survive and thrive, I had to learn to prioritize strategically and communicate transparently with both staff and administration.

This challenge is universal. A hospital unit manager, for example, balances administrative mandates for efficiency with nurses' needs for adequate patient care time. To succeed, they might use a prioritization matrix to distinguish urgent tasks (e.g., compliance reports) from important ones (e.g., staff training). Strategic prioritization ensures alignment without sacrificing team morale.

Practical Tips:

- **Use Prioritization Frameworks**: Separate urgent from essential tasks.

- **Block Time for Strategic Thinking:** Protect time to focus on long-term goals.

- **Communicate Transparently:** Explain why priorities shift to maintain trust and alignment.

Expanded Strategy: The Decision-Making Compass

To enhance prioritization, middle leaders can use a "Decision-Making Compass," a framework that evaluates tasks based on impact, urgency, and alignment with goals. For instance, a retail manager facing competing demands, restocking inventory vs. training new hires, might score tasks on a 1–5 scale for each criterion, prioritizing those with the highest combined score. This approach, tested in a logistics firm, reduced operational delays by 15% by focusing on high-impact tasks.

2. Leading Without Full Authority

At Lifehouse Daniel Academy, I supervised teaching staff, daycare staff, and students while also teaching middle and high school classes. I was accountable for outcomes but lacked absolute control over every decision.

For instance, implementing curriculum changes or staffing adjustments required persuasion and collaboration rather than command and control. Through this experience, I realized that influence, not authority, determines success in the middle.

By mentoring staff, listening to concerns, and fostering a shared vision, I helped the school grow enrollment by **25%** in two years. Leadership, I discovered, is less about the title and more about inspiring others to follow willingly.

This challenge is evident in many contexts. A marketing team lead at a startup, lacking budget control, persuaded executives to fund a new campaign by presenting data-driven results from a pilot, increasing conversions by **20%.** Influence relies on trust, empathy, and strategic communication.

Practical Tips:

- Build trust by following through on commitments.
- Develop emotional intelligence to influence without authority.
- Frame initiatives in terms of team and organizational benefits.

Expanded Strategy: The Influence Matrix

To build influence, middle leaders can use an "Influence Matrix" to map stakeholders (e.g., team, peers, executives) and identify their motivations (e.g., career growth, efficiency). By customizing communication, emphasizing team benefits to staff and ROI to executives, leaders can gain buy-in. A nonprofit coordinator used this approach to align volunteers and board members, increasing event attendance by **30%.**

3. Managing Up and Down Simultaneously

As General Manager at Revolution Fitness, I was responsible for both day-to-day operations and strategic partnerships. I advocated for my staff's needs for senior leadership while ensuring the team executed executive directives.

Mornings often began with negotiating resources and corporate executives, and by afternoon, I was motivating staff on the floor. Credibility with both sides required honesty, clear communication, and careful documentation. By bridging these worlds, I helped grow monthly revenue from **$25,000** to **$60,000** in six months while maintaining morale and performance.

This dual role is common. A city planner managing a community project might negotiate funding with municipal leaders while rallying residents for support. Success hinges on maintaining open communication channels and aligning expectations.

Practical Tips:

- Maintain open communication with leadership and staff.

- Set clear expectations and priorities.

- Document challenges and achievements to strengthen advocacy.

Expanded Strategy: The Two-Way Communication Framework

Middle leaders can adopt a "Two-Way Communication Framework" to manage up and down. This involves weekly check-ins with teams to clarify goals and monthly reports to executives summarizing progress and needs. A logistics supervisor used this framework to align drivers and management, reducing delivery errors by **10%.**

4. Navigating Organizational Politics

During my time as Owner/Operator of two Wingzone franchises, I managed a diverse staff, coordinated with corporate vendors, and implemented marketing strategies.

Each stakeholder, staff member, vendor, and corporate partner had competing priorities, and navigating these relationships required diplomacy and awareness.

Middle leaders must anticipate conflicts, influence outcomes subtly, and maintain credibility while fostering collaboration and teamwork. Missteps can alienate staff or partners; skillful navigation can unlock resources and opportunities. By listening actively, building alliances, and remaining neutral when necessary, I maintained strong relationships and successfully grew the business.

For example, a tech firm's project manager navigated tensions between developers and sales teams by hosting joint planning sessions, aligning priorities, and boosting project completion rates by **15%.** Diplomacy and strategic alliances are key to navigating politics.

Practical Tips:

- Observe and listen to understand motivations.

- Build alliances across departments and stakeholders.

- Stay neutral when necessary to maintain credibility.

Expanded Strategy: The Stakeholder Alignment Map

A "Stakeholder Alignment Map" helps middle leaders navigate politics by plotting stakeholders' interests, influence, and potential conflicts. By identifying overlap (e.g., shared goals) and addressing tensions (e.g., competing priorities), leaders can foster collaboration.

A school administrator used this map to align teachers and parents, improving student outcomes by **12%**.

5. Developing Talent While Managing Performance

Coaching high school football and basketball taught me a vital lesson: performance and development must go hand in hand. Leading championship-winning teams required balancing rigorous athletic training with mentoring players academically and personally.

Similarly, as a department head, I supported teachers' professional growth while making sure student learning outcomes were met. Individual development plans, delegated responsibilities, and recognition of progress helped me cultivate both talent and performance.

This balance is critical in other settings. A retail manager mentored cashiers while maintaining sales targets, reducing turnover by **15%** through personalized coaching. Development fosters loyalty and performance.

Practical Tips:

- Create individual development plans for team members.
- Delegate tasks that challenge and grow skills.
- Recognize and celebrate progress to motivate continued improvement.

Expanded Strategy: The Talent Development Cycle

Middle leaders can use a "Talent Development Cycle" with four phases: assess strengths, set goals, provide opportunities, and review progress. A healthcare supervisor implemented this cycle, assigning nurses to lead training sessions, improving team skills and patient care metrics by **10%**.

6. Managing Change and Uncertainty

Starting a daycare program at Lifehouse Daniel Academy presented a whirlwind of challenges, including regulatory compliance, staffing, curriculum development, and preparing for the first school year.

At Lifehouse Daniel Academmy, change was constant, and uncertainty could have easily overwhelmed the team. Breaking tasks into manageable steps, involving staff in the planning process, and communicating clearly helped maintain morale and ensure success. Modeling calm, adaptive behavior allowed the team to thrive even in uncertain conditions.

Similarly, a manufacturing team lead managed a factory's transition to automated systems by breaking the process into phases, involving workers in training, and maintaining open communication, reducing downtime by **20%**.

Practical Tips:

- Communicate early and frequently about changes.
- Involve the team in planning to build buy-in.
- Break large projects into smaller, achievable steps to reduce overwhelm.

Expanded Strategy: The Change Management Roadmap

A "Change Management Roadmap" guides teams through transitions with steps: communicate the vision, engage stakeholders, implement incrementally, and monitor outcomes. A nonprofit leader used this roadmap to launch a new program, increasing community participation by **25%**.

7. Handling Criticism and Conflict

Middle leaders are often the first to receive complaints. Managing criticism well requires objectivity, emotional intelligence, and conflict resolution skills.

A biblical example: Moses' officials faithfully handled disputes under his guidance.

Practical Tip: Use the "listen, clarify, act" method to address criticism constructively.

For instance, a customer service manager faced complaints about response times. By listening to staff concerns, clarifying expectations, and implementing a new ticketing system, response times improved by 15%. This approach turns criticism into an opportunity.

Expanded Strategy: The Conflict Resolution Framework

A "Conflict Resolution Framework" involves listening actively, identifying root causes, proposing solutions, and following up. A school principal used this to resolve parent-teacher disputes, improving satisfaction by 20%.

8. Avoiding Burnout

High-pressure demands increase the risk of burnout. Gallup studies indicate that middle managers experience some of the highest burnout rates, directly affecting team performance.

A biblical example: Jesus withdrew for prayer and rest (*Mark 1:35*), modeling the importance of renewal. Practical Tip: Establish personal rhythms of rest and renewal, including breaks, reflection, and professional boundaries.

A tech manager avoided burnout by scheduling weekly reflection time and delegating tasks, maintaining team productivity during a high-pressure project.

Expanded Strategy: The Resilience Plan

A "Resilience Plan" includes daily breaks, weekly reflection, and monthly professional development. A retail manager implemented this plan, reducing stress and improving team morale by **15%**.

Biblical Perspective

Exodus **18:13–27** illustrates Moses' challenge as a middle leader. Overwhelmed by handling all disputes alone, Moses was advised by Jethro to delegate responsibilities to capable leaders. This example highlights the importance of discerning where to act personally and where to empower others, striking a balance between responsibility and authority.

Another biblical example is David (*1 Samuel 18–20*), who navigated Saul's court with integrity, managing conflicts and building alliances despite lacking ultimate authority. His resilience and faith offer a model for middle leaders facing political and interpersonal challenges.

Global Perspectives on Middle Leadership Challenges

Challenges vary across cultures. In collectivist cultures like India, middle leaders prioritize group harmony, as seen when a factory manager facilitated consensus to implement a new process, improving efficiency by **15%.** In individualist cultures like Australia, assertiveness is key, as a startup manager demonstrated by advocating for team resources, securing a **10%** budget increase.

A case study from South Africa shows a community health coordinator navigating politics to align stakeholders, boosting program participation by **20%.** Cultural sensitivity enhances middle leaders' ability to address challenges effectively.

Weekly Plan of Action: Navigating Middle Leadership Challenges

This seven-day plan helps middle leaders address the chapter's challenges, building resilience, influence, and team alignment. Each day focuses on a specific action tied to a challenge, with measurable goals and reflection prompts.

Day 1: Prioritize Strategically

- **Action:** Use Eisenhower's Urgent-Important Matrix to list your week's tasks. Prioritize one high-impact task and delegate a low-priority one.
- **Goal:** Focus on what drives results.
- **Reflection:** Did prioritization improve efficiency? What task can you delegate next?

Day 2: Build Influence

- **Action**: Identify a stakeholder (e.g., team member, executive) and have a conversation to understand their priorities. Frame a suggestion to align with their goals.
- **Goal:** Strengthen influence through empathy.
- **Reflection:** How did they respond? How can you refine your approach?

Day 3: Manage Up and Down

- **Action:** Schedule a brief check-in with your team to clarify a goal and email a concise update to your supervisor, highlighting progress and needs.
- **Goal:** Align communication across levels.
- **Reflection:** Did communication improve clarity? What adjustments are needed?

Day 4: Navigate Politics

- **Action:** Map one stakeholder relationship (e.g., a peer) using the Stakeholder Alignment Map. Identify their motivations and propose a collaborative idea.
- **Goal:** Build a strategic alliance.
- **Reflection:** Did the interaction foster collaboration? What's the next step?

Day 5: Develop Talent

- **Action:** Create a development plan for one team member, assigning a task that stretches their skills (e.g., leading a meeting). Provide feedback afterward.
- **Goal:** Foster growth and performance.
- **Reflection:** How did they respond? What support do they need?

Day 6: Manage Change

- **Action**: Identify an upcoming change (e.g., new process). Break it into three actionable steps and communicate one to your team, inviting input.
- **Goal**: Build buy-in for change.
- **Reflection:** Did involving the team reduce resistance? How can you improve?

Day 7: Prevent Burnout

- **Action:** Schedule 30 minutes for reflection or rest. Journal one lesson from the week and set a goal to address a challenge (e.g., delegation, communication).
- **Goal:** Build resilience.
- **Reflection:** How did rest impact your focus? What's your next goal?

This plan empowers middle leaders to tackle challenges systematically, enhancing their impact.

Key Takeaways

Middle leadership is demanding but pivotal. Balancing priorities, influencing without authority, and handling conflict are core challenges. Biblical leaders demonstrate strategies for navigating tension with wisdom. Burnout is preventable through intentional rest and delegation. Middle leaders have the power to transform teams, organizations, and communities by navigating challenges with insight, faith, and resilience.

Reflection Questions

- Which challenge of middle leadership resonates most with your experience?
- How can you manage competing priorities more effectively?
- What strategies can you implement to maintain balance and prevent burnout?

Conclusion

Middle leadership is a crucible of challenges, but it's also a platform for profound impact. By navigating competing priorities, leading without authority, managing up and down, handling politics, developing talent, embracing change, resolving conflicts, and preventing burnout, middle leaders shape their organizations' success. With faith, wisdom, and practical strategies, they turn challenges into opportunities, leaving a legacy of growth and transformation.

"The middle of the road is where the yellow line is, and it's also where the vision begins."

— Adapted proverb

"For I know the plans I have for you," declares the Lord, "plans to prosper you and not to harm you, plans to give you hope and a future."
— Jeremiah 29:11

Chapter 3:
Opportunities Hidden in the Middle

Chapter 2 illuminated the complex challenges of middle leadership, balancing competing priorities, leading without full authority, navigating politics, and managing change while avoiding burnout. These demands test resilience and wisdom, but they also set the stage for extraordinary opportunities.

Middle leaders are positioned at the intersection of vision and execution. They are uniquely equipped to transform challenges into catalysts for growth, innovation, and impact. This chapter shifts focus to the hidden opportunities within the middle, opportunities to innovate, connect, mentor, and shape organizational culture.

By leveraging their vantage point, organizations can assist middle leaders in turning obstacles into stepping stones, creating lasting value for their teams, organizations, and themselves.

Introduction

Middle leadership is often portrayed as a role fraught with challenges: managing competing priorities, leading without full authority, and bridging the gap between senior leadership and frontline teams. Even though these challenges are real, with the proper support, they obscure the unique opportunities this position affords.

Middle leaders occupy a vantage point few other roles provide; they can see the broad organizational vision while remaining intimately familiar with the operational realities on the ground. This dual perspective allows middle leaders to identify gaps, anticipate problems, and propose practical solutions that create measurable impact.

They become translators of strategy, problem-solvers of operational bottlenecks, and innovators of new approaches. Beyond processes and systems, middle leaders have a profound influence on culture. Their daily interactions with teams, which are combined with access to upper management, allow them to model behaviors, inspire values, and shape engagement and morale.

Middle leadership is also a space for personal and professional growth. Operating in this role requires adaptability, emotional intelligence, and strategic thinking. Leaders develop influence through relationships rather than hierarchy, learning to navigate ambiguity while fostering collaboration and accountability.

Those who embrace the middle fully often emerge more resilient, insightful, and impactful than leaders at any other level. The middle management is where influence, innovation, and personal development intersect, revealing opportunities often hidden from both the top and bottom of the organizational ladder.

The Strategic Advantage of the Middle

Middle leaders are uniquely positioned to see both the forest and the trees, along with the big-picture goals of the organization and the daily realities of execution. This dual perspective is a strategic advantage, enabling them to identify opportunities that others might miss. A **2024** Harvard Business Review study found that middle leaders who make use of their position to propose solutions increase team productivity by **22%** and organizational agility by **18%**. Their proximity to operations allows them to spot inefficiencies, while their connection to leadership ensures alignment with strategic goals.

For example, a logistics coordinator at a global retailer noticed delays in inventory restocking. By proposing a real-time tracking system and aligning it with corporate goals, they reduced restocking time by **20%**, improving customer satisfaction. This ability to connect operational insights with strategic objectives makes middle leaders indispensable catalysts for change.

Opportunity 1: Driving Innovation

Middle leaders are uniquely positioned to observe operational realities that executives may not be able to see. They can identify inefficiencies, gaps, and opportunities for creative solutions that can effortlessly improve processes, enhance outcomes, and add value across the organization.

Example: While serving as General Manager at Revolution Fitness, I noticed delays in client onboarding. These delays were frustrating for new members and contributed to higher-than-necessary drop-off rates. I redesigned the process using digital intake forms, automated follow-ups, and personalized orientation sessions to enhance efficiency and effectiveness. The result was faster onboarding, higher client retention, and a staff that was freed up to focus on delivering high-quality training. This demonstrates how middle-level insight transforms bottlenecks into opportunities for innovation and growth.

Expanded Example: In a healthcare setting, a nurse manager observed long patient wait times due to manual scheduling. By introducing an automated scheduling tool and training staff, they reduced wait times by **25%,** improving patient satisfaction and staff morale. This innovation, born from the middle leader's proximity to operations, demonstrates their role as change agents.

Practical Tips for Driving Creativity:

- Observe operational workflows for inefficiencies or recurring pain points.
- Suggest solutions that are practical, actionable, and aligned with organizational goals.
- Advocate for new ideas by presenting clear evidence of potential impact.
- Encourage experimentation and small-scale pilots to test innovations safely.

Expanded Strategy: The Innovation Spark Framework

The "Innovation Spark Framework" helps middle leaders drive innovation systematically: (1) Observe (identify pain points), (2) Ideate (brainstorm solutions), (3) Pilot (test small-scale), and (4) Scale (implement broadly). A manufacturing supervisor used this framework to streamline quality checks, reducing defects by **15%**. You can easily apply it by mapping one process and proposing a pilot solution.

Reflective Exercise: Identify one process or system in your team that could be improved. How could you redesign it for efficiency or better outcomes?

Opportunity 2: Building Bridges Across Boundaries

Middle leaders have the ability to naturally connect teams, departments, and individuals who might otherwise operate in silos. They have the influence to foster collaboration, streamline communication, and create organizational alignment.

Example: At Revolution Fitness, the marketing, sales, and training teams often worked independently, resulting in miscommunication and inefficiency. I organized cross-department meetings and implemented shared communication channels. This visibility allowed teams to coordinate on promotions, client onboarding, and operational priorities, fostering collaboration and accountability.

Expanded Example: In a tech startup, a product manager bridged developers and sales teams by creating a shared dashboard for project updates, reducing miscommunication and speeding up product launches by **20%.** This bridge-building role enhances efficiency and trust across departments.

Practical Tips for Building Bridges:

- Schedule regular cross-team meetings to encourage dialogue.
- Create shared digital spaces for transparent communication.
- Recognize and reward collaborative efforts to reinforce team alignment.
- Facilitate informal relationship-building activities to strengthen interpersonal trust.

Expanded Strategy For The Collaboration Connector Model

The "Collaboration Connector Model" involves mapping interdependencies, identifying communication gaps, and creating channels for alignment. A nonprofit coordinator implemented this model to align volunteers and staff, increasing event participation by **25%**. Apply it by charting key stakeholders and scheduling a cross-team meeting.

Reflective Exercise: Map the interdependencies between your team and other departments to ensure effective collaboration. Where can stronger connections create better outcomes?

Opportunity 3: Developing Talent and Mentoring Others

Middle leaders have a front-row seat to talent development. By recognizing strengths, offering guidance, and providing growth opportunities, they enhance individual and team performance while cultivating future leaders.

Example: As Assistant Varsity Football and Basketball Coach at John Curtis Christian School, I mentored athletes not only in skills and performance but also in discipline, confidence, and leadership. Structured coaching, feedback, and encouragement helped athletes achieve championships while preparing them for life beyond sports. Similarly, mentoring teachers in educational settings can enhance instructional practices, morale, and professional growth.

Expanded Example: A retail manager mentored a cashier to lead a sales initiative, boosting team revenue by **10%** and preparing the cashier for a supervisory role. This dual focus on performance and development creates a pipeline of future leaders.

Practical Tips for Talent Development:

- Create individualized development plans to guide growth.
- Provide ongoing feedback, coaching, and opportunities for skill-building.
- Celebrate progress and achievements to reinforce motivation.
- Encourage autonomy and problem-solving to foster leadership potential.

Expanded Strategy: The Talent Growth Cycle

The "Talent Growth Cycle" includes assessing strengths, setting goals, providing stretch assignments, and reviewing progress. A healthcare supervisor used this cycle to assign nurses to lead training, improving patient care metrics by 12%. Apply it by drafting a development plan for one team member.

Reflective Exercise: Choose one team member to mentor this quarter. What skills or habits can you help them develop?

Opportunity 4: Driving Operational Improvements

Middle leaders usually have the clearest view of daily operations, which allows them to implement improvements that enhance efficiency, reduce errors, and improve outcomes.

Example: At Lifehouse Daniel Academy, I observed inefficiencies in student enrollment and classroom scheduling. By creating standardized procedures, implementing tracking tools, and optimizing schedules, I reduced errors and freed staff to focus on meaningful student engagement. Operational improvements not only streamline workflows but also foster a productive and motivated work environment.

Expanded Example: A logistics coordinator at a distribution center noticed delays in order processing. By introducing a barcode scanning system and retraining staff, they reduced processing time by **18%,** boosting customer satisfaction. This demonstrates the middle leader's ability to drive tangible improvements.

Practical Tips for Operational Improvement:

- Map current processes and identify bottlenecks.
- Introduce tools or protocols that streamline workflows.
- Involve staff in designing improvements to gain buy-in and insights.
- Monitor outcomes and adjust processes as needed.

Expanded Strategy: The Process Optimization Blueprint

The "Process Optimization Blueprint" involves mapping workflows, identifying inefficiencies, testing solutions, and monitoring results. A manufacturing team lead used this blueprint to streamline assembly lines, increasing output by **15%**. Apply it by auditing one process and proposing a solution.

Reflective Exercise: What daily processes in your team could be improved with minor adjustments or technology enhancements?

Opportunity 5: Influencing Culture and Morale

Policies or mission statements do not define culture; daily interactions and consistent behavior shape it. Middle leaders wield significant influence over organizational culture because they engage directly and consistently with teams.

Example: As Owner/Operator of Wingzone, I cultivated a culture of accountability, teamwork, and customer service excellence. Recognizing employee achievements and providing constructive coaching reinforced desired behaviors, enhanced morale, and encouraged loyalty. A strong, positive culture motivates employees to excel and creates a foundation for long-term business success.

Expanded Example: A school administrator fostered a culture of collaboration by recognizing teacher contributions publicly and addressing conflicts promptly, improving retention by **20%**. This shows how middle leaders shape culture through intentional actions.

Practical Tips for Shaping Culture:

- Model organizational values consistently through words and actions.
- Celebrate achievements to reinforce desired behaviors.
- Address issues promptly to maintain trust and morale.
- Encourage collaboration and recognize contributions publicly.

Expanded Strategy: The Culture Builder Framework

The "Culture Builder Framework" involves defining desired values, modeling them, reinforcing them through recognition, and addressing misalignments. A nonprofit leader used this framework to foster inclusivity, increasing volunteer engagement by **22%.** Apply it by identifying one value to reinforce and modeling it daily.

Reflective Exercise: What cultural behaviors do you want to reinforce in your team? How can you model them daily?

Opportunity 6: Serving as a Strategic

Link Middle leaders are the bridge between strategy and execution. They translate broad organizational objectives into actionable plans, identify obstacles, and communicate feedback to ensure alignment and smooth implementation.

Example: At Revolution Fitness, I converted corporate growth strategies into daily operational plans, coordinated team execution, and monitored progress. Acting as the strategic link ensured both leadership and staff understood goals, anticipated challenges, and executed initiatives effectively.

Expanded Example: A tech project manager translated a CEO's vision for a new product into actionable sprints, communicating progress to executives and clarifying tasks for developers, resulting in a **20%** faster launch. This role ensures alignment and impact.

Practical Tips for Serving as a Strategic Link:

- Translate high-level strategy into clear, actionable steps for your team.

- Communicate consistently, upward and downward, to maintain alignment.

- Identify obstacles early and propose practical solutions.

- Ensure that teams understand how their contributions connect to organizational objectives.

Expanded Strategy: The Strategy Alignment Matrix

The "Strategy Alignment Matrix" maps organizational goals to team tasks, identifying gaps and solutions. A retail manager used this matrix to align staff efforts with sales goals, increasing revenue by a whopping **15%**. You can also apply it by mapping one goal to team actions.

Reflective Exercise: Choose a current organizational initiative. How can you clarify its purpose and translate it into actionable steps for your team?

Additional Opportunities: Creativity, Influence, and Legacy

Beyond operational and strategic contributions, middle leaders can leverage the middle space to:

- **Foster Creativity:** Encourage experimentation and new ideas, providing a safe space for innovation.
- **Expand Influence:** Build networks and credibility across teams and departments, creating lasting impact.
- **Leave a Legacy:** Shape processes, culture, and talent development in ways that endure long after projects conclude.

For example, a community health coordinator fostered creativity by just encouraging his staff to propose outreach ideas, leading to a campaign that increased participation by **25%**. A finance team lead expanded influence by collaborating with sales, improving budget accuracy. These are small efforts, but they have the power to create a lasting legacy.

Biblical Perspective: Timothy's Example

Scripture offers insight into middle leadership opportunities through Timothy (**1 Timothy 4:12**). As a young leader, Timothy influenced older peers through example, faith, and action, mentoring others despite lacking supreme authority. His story shows how middle leaders can shape culture, develop talent, and drive impact through influence and integrity, inspiring modern leaders to seize similar opportunities.

Global Perspectives on Middle Leadership Opportunities

Just like one example does not fit all, opportunities also vary across cultures, companies, etc. In collectivist cultures like Japan, middle leaders foster collaboration through consensus, as seen when a factory manager aligned teams for a new process, improving efficiency by **15%**. In individualist cultures like the U.S., they drive innovation through bold proposals, as a startup manager did to secure funding for a project. A Brazilian nonprofit leader bridged community and board priorities, boosting program impact by **20%**. Cultural sensitivity amplifies opportunities.

Weekly Plan of Action: Seizing Middle Leadership Opportunities

This seven-day plan helps middle leaders apply to all the above-mentioned opportunities, focusing on innovation, collaboration, and impact. Each day targets a specific opportunity with actionable steps and reflection prompts.

Day 1: Spark Innovation

- **Action:** Identify one inefficient process in your team. Propose a small-scale solution using the Innovation Spark Framework (e.g., a new tool or streamlined step).
- **Goal:** Drive incremental improvement.
- **Reflection:** What was the initial response? How can you refine your idea?

Day 2: Build Bridges

- **Action:** Schedule a meeting with another department to discuss a shared goal using the Collaboration Connector Model. Create a shared communication channel.
- **Goal:** Foster cross-team alignment.
- **Reflection:** Did collaboration improve? What connections need strengthening?

Day 3: Develop Talent

- **Action:** Draft a development plan for one team member using the Talent Growth Cycle. Assign a stretch task (e.g., leading a task) and provide feedback.
- **Goal:** Enhance skills and performance.
- **Reflection:** How did they respond? What support is needed?

Day 4: Optimize Operations

- **Action:** Audit one workflow using the Process Optimization Blueprint. Propose one improvement and involve your team in planning it.
- **Goal:** Streamline operations.
- **Reflection:** Did the improvement reduce inefficiencies? What's next?

Day 5: Shape Culture

- **Action:** Model one desired value (e.g., collaboration) using the Culture Builder Framework. Recognize a team member's contribution publicly.
- **Goal:** Reinforce positive culture.
- **Reflection:** Did your actions influence team behavior? How can you sustain it?

Day 6: Align Strategy

- **Action:** Choose an organizational goal and use the Strategy Alignment Matrix to break it into three team tasks. Communicate the "why" to your team.
- **Goal**: Ensure strategic alignment.
- **Reflection:** Did your team understand the goal's purpose? How can you clarify further?

Day 7: Reflect and Plan

- **Action:** Schedule 30 minutes to journal one lesson from the week and set a goal to seize an opportunity (e.g., innovation, mentoring) using one framework.

- **Goal:** Consolidate learning and plan growth.

- **Reflection:** How did this week's actions enhance your impact? What's your next step?

This plan empowers middle leaders to seize opportunities systematically, maximizing their influence.

Conclusion

Middle leadership is often misperceived as a constrained role, defined by limitations. In truth, it is a position rich with opportunities: to innovate, collaborate, mentor, improve operations, influence culture, and bridge strategy and execution. Leaders who embrace their vantage point can turn challenges into opportunities, translating vision into action while leaving a lasting organizational impact.

The middle is also a place for profound personal growth. Navigating complex challenges sharpens emotional intelligence, problem-solving skills, and strategic thinking. Middle leaders develop influence through relationships, grow resilience, and cultivate leadership skills that prepare them for broader roles. Leadership in the middle is not about authority; it is about intentional influence, insight, and action. Those who embrace it fully can transform organizations, nurture talent, and shape culture, leaving a legacy that extends far beyond any title or position.

"Vision without execution is just hallucination."
— Thomas Edison

"Where there is no vision, the people perish."
— Proverbs 29:18

Chapter 4:
Vision Carriers and Translators

Chapter 3 illuminated the hidden opportunities within middle leadership, driving innovation, building bridges, mentoring talent, and shaping culture. These opportunities empower middle leaders to transform their organizations from a unique vantage point. Yet, to fully realize this potential, middle leaders must master the art of carrying and translating vision.

By connecting high-level strategies to daily actions, they ensure that opportunities translate into tangible results. This chapter explores how middle leaders serve as vision carriers and translators, turning abstract strategy into actionable plans, fostering alignment, and inspiring teams to achieve organizational goals with purpose and impact.

Introduction

Middle leaders hold a unique and indispensable role in organizations: they are both carriers and translators of vision. While senior executives define overarching strategies and long-term objectives, middle leaders ensure these directives are not just abstract ideas but actionable realities. Without middle leaders translating vision into concrete plans, even the clearest corporate strategies can falter.

This dual responsibility requires a combination and a precise balance of strategic understanding, communication skills, and emotional intelligence. Middle leaders must engage, inspire, and guide teams while simultaneously balancing operational demands and organizational expectations. Research from Harvard Business Review suggests that companies with middle leaders who excel at seamlessly translating vision into practical objectives experience **1.5** times higher employee engagement and are twice as likely to achieve their strategic goals.

In essence, middle leaders serve as the connective tissue between vision and execution, binding strategy to action in ways that determine an organization's success.

In my experience across education, business, athletics, and ministry, I've seen firsthand how middle leaders transform abstract strategies into tangible results. In schools, they guide teachers through curriculum changes; in businesses, they implement growth plans with precision; in athletics, they turn coaching strategies into winning plays. Middle leaders are often the unsung heroes whose work ensures that vision becomes reality.

The Strategic Role of Vision Translation

Middle leaders are the linchpins of organizational success, translating high-level vision into actionable outcomes. A **2025** McKinsey study found that organizations with effective middle leadership achieve **30%** higher strategic alignment and **20%** greater employee engagement. Their ability to bridge executive intent with operational execution ensures strategies don't remain abstract but drive measurable results.

For example, a supply chain manager at a retail firm translated a corporate goal of reducing costs into optimized delivery routes, cutting expenses by **15%** while maintaining service quality. This strategic role requires clarity, adaptability, and influence, positioning middle leaders as critical drivers of organizational progress.

The Importance of "Why"

Before employees can fully commit to goals, they must understand the "why" behind the work. Why does this task matter? Why is this goal important? Understanding the purpose behind assignments gives employees context, motivation, and a sense of ownership. Simon Sinek's research highlights that individuals are far more inspired and committed when they understand the purpose driving their work. Middle leaders act as the conduit for this understanding, translating strategic intent into a rationale that resonates with their teams. They are bound to show employees that their contributions are meaningful, connecting daily tasks to the larger organizational objectives. Without this clarity, even well-defined goals can feel arbitrary, leaving teams disengaged or demotivated.

Communicating the "why" also fosters creativity and initiative. Employees who understand the purpose behind their work are more likely to identify opportunities for improvement, develop innovative solutions, and align their efforts with broader organizational objectives. They move from simply completing tasks to actively contributing to organizational success.

Expanded Example: In a nonprofit, a program coordinator explained how a new outreach initiative would provide meals to 500 families, connecting staff tasks to community impact. This clarity boosted volunteer engagement by **25%,** as team members felt their work had purpose by framing functions within the "why." Middle leaders ignite motivation and innovation.

Carrying Vision Downward

Once the "why" is established, middle leaders focus on helping teams understand how goals translate into daily work, why tasks matter, and what success looks like.

Why Goals Matter

Middle leaders motivate teams by articulating the significance of individual goals. In a healthcare setting, for example, implementing a new patient data system is not just a technological upgrade; it enables safer, faster patient care. By framing goals in terms of real-world impact, middle leaders give employees a sense of purpose. Organizational psychology research confirms that employees who grasp the "why" behind their tasks demonstrate higher initiative, accountability, and performance.

Expanded Example: A school administrator explained how a new curriculum aligned with state standards would improve student outcomes, motivating teachers to adopt it, resulting in a 10% increase in test scores. This clarity transforms tasks into meaningful contributions.

How Tasks Connect to Mission

Middle leaders also translate strategic objectives into concrete and actionable steps. A marketing manager tasked with expanding into a new region, for example, relies on the middle leader to break this goal into assignments, deadlines, and measurable outcomes. This clarity reduces confusion, prevents misaligned efforts, and fosters alignment with organizational priorities.

Expanded Example: In a tech firm, a project manager broke a CEO's goal of launching a new app into development sprints, marketing campaigns, and user testing phases, ensuring a **20%** faster launch. This translation ensures alignment and efficiency.

Defining Success

Finally, middle leaders define what success looks like. Goals without clear benchmarks often lead to effort without impact. For instance, in software development, success might include timely code delivery, user satisfaction, cross-team collaboration, and maintainable solutions. By establishing both quantitative and qualitative indicators, middle leaders help teams align their efforts with organizational values and strategic priorities.

Expanded Example: A retail manager defined success for a sales initiative as a **15%** revenue increase and improved customer feedback, providing clear metrics that guided team efforts and achieved both goals. Clear benchmarks drive focused action.

Translating Vision Across Boundaries

Middle leaders do more than cascade vision downward; they also translate it laterally, across teams and departments. Strategic objectives often require adaptation for different functions, and middle leaders ensure the vision resonates without losing its intent. A retail company aiming to enhance customer experience, for example, must adjust its strategy differently for logistics, marketing, and IT teams. Middle leaders bridge these perspectives, clarifying responsibilities and aligning efforts to ensure a cohesive approach. This approach minimizes friction, fosters collaboration, and cultivates a shared sense of purpose across diverse teams.

Practical methods include facilitating cross-departmental meetings, establishing transparent communication channels, and encouraging team members to share their insights and feedback. By doing so, middle leaders ensure that strategy is implemented holistically rather than in isolated silos.

Expanded Example: In a manufacturing firm, a production supervisor aligned quality control and sales teams by hosting joint planning sessions, reducing product defects by 12% and boosting customer satisfaction. This cross-boundary translation ensures cohesive execution.

Practical Insights and Real-Life Examples

Effective middle leaders employ storytelling, coaching, and feedback to carry and translate vision. A nonprofit manager, for instance, might explain how fundraising efforts directly enable community programs. In corporate settings, leaders share success stories from other teams to illustrate practical applications of strategy.

A biblical example can be found in Nehemiah (Nehemiah 2–6). Nehemiah received a vision to rebuild Jerusalem's walls but relied on leaders at multiple levels to motivate workers, clarify objectives, assign tasks, and communicate expectations. This demonstrates that effective vision translation is both timeless and practical.

Other real-world examples include:

- In education, department heads translate school-wide academic goals into lesson plans, assessments, and mentoring strategies for teachers.

- In business, project managers take executive growth plans and convert them into operational workflows, KPIs, and team assignments.

- In sports, assistant coaches turn head coaching strategies into drills, plays, and performance objectives for players.

Expanded Example: At a community health organization, a coordinator translated a board's goal of expanding outreach into targeted campaigns, training volunteers, and tracking impact, increasing participation by 22%. Storytelling and clear metrics drove success.

Challenges in Carrying and Translating Vision

Middle leaders face unique challenges in this role:

Conflicting Priorities

Balancing competing goals from executives and team needs requires discernment and careful consideration. Middle leaders must decide where to allocate time, energy, and resources while maintaining alignment with both strategy and operational realities.

Expanded Example: A logistics manager balanced corporate demands for cost-cutting with team needs for equipment upgrades, negotiating a phased approach that saved **10%** while maintaining efficiency. Discernment ensures alignment without sacrifice.

Resistance to Change

Teams may hesitate to adopt new initiatives. Middle leaders require emotional intelligence, empathy, and active listening to handle resistance while keeping momentum.

Expanded Example: A school principal faced teacher resistance to a new grading system. By hosting feedback sessions and explaining benefits, they achieved **90%** adoption, improving grading consistency. Empathy turns resistance into buy-in.

Maintaining Motivation

Sustaining enthusiasm during setbacks or extended projects is crucial. Celebrating milestones, recognizing contributions, and communicating progress help maintain engagement and morale.

Expanded Example: A tech team lead kept developers motivated during a delayed project by celebrating small wins, resulting in on-time delivery and high team morale. Recognition sustains momentum.

Strategies to Overcome Challenges

- Reinforce the "why" regularly: Remind teams of the purpose behind their work.

- Encourage two-way communication: Listen to feedback to identify gaps in understanding and improve execution.

- Tailor messages: Adapt vision communication to different team cultures and operational realities.

- Celebrate milestones: Recognize achievements to sustain motivation and momentum.

Expanded Strategy: The Vision Translation Framework

The "Vision Translation Framework" involves four steps: (1) Clarify (understand the vision), (2) Communicate (share the "why"), (3) Operationalize (break into tasks), and (4) Monitor (track progress and adjust). A retail manager used this framework to align a sales team with a growth strategy, increasing revenue by **15%.** Apply it by mapping one goal to actionable steps.

The Middle Leader as a Culture Builder

In addition to translating vision, middle leaders shape organizational culture. By modeling behaviors, reinforcing values, and celebrating successes, they cultivate trust, engagement, and accountability. The way they communicate, respond to challenges, and recognize contributions sets the tone for the broader team. In my experience, middle leaders who act intentionally as culture builders create environments where employees feel empowered, connected, and motivated. Teams are not only productive but also resilient, innovative, and aligned with organizational goals.

Expanded Example: A hospital supervisor fostered a culture of patient-centered care by modeling empathy and recognizing staff efforts, improving patient satisfaction scores by **18%.** Intentional actions shape lasting culture.

Biblical Perspective: Joseph's Example

Scripture offers insight through Joseph (**Genesis 41**), who translated Pharaoh's vision of preparing for famine into actionable plans, organizing grain storage and distribution. His clarity, communication, and execution show how middle leaders turn vision into reality, inspiring modern leaders to do the same.

Global Perspectives on Vision Translation

Vision translation varies across cultures. In collectivist cultures like China, middle leaders emphasize group alignment, as a factory manager did to implement a new process, improving efficiency by **15%.** In individualist cultures like the U.S., they focus on clear communication, as a startup manager did to align teams, speeding up a product launch by **20%.** A Brazilian nonprofit leader tailored messaging to diverse stakeholders, boosting program impact by **18%.** Cultural sensitivity enhances vision translation.

Weekly Plan of Action: Carrying and Translating Vision

This seven-day plan helps middle leaders apply the above shared principles, focusing on communicating purpose, aligning tasks, and overcoming challenges. Each day targets a specific aspect with actionable steps and reflection prompts.

Day 1: Clarify the Vision

- **Action:** Review one organizational goal and use the Vision Translation Framework to clarify its "why." Write a one-sentence summary of its purpose.
- **Goal:** Understand the vision deeply.
- **Reflection:** Did clarifying the "why" enhance your understanding? How can you refine it?

Day 2: Communicate the "Why"

- **Action:** Share the "why" of the goal with your team in a meeting or email, emphasizing its impact (e.g., customer benefit, team growth).
- **Goal:** Inspire team motivation.
- **Reflection:** Did the team connect with the purpose? How can you improve communication?

Day 3: Break Down Tasks

- **Action:** Use the Vision Translation Framework to break the goal into three actionable tasks for your team. Assign responsibilities and deadlines.
- **Goal:** Create clear, actionable steps.
- **Reflection:** Did the tasks align with the goal? What adjustments are needed?

Day 4: Foster Cross-Team Alignment

- **Action:** Meet with another department to align on the goal, using shared communication channels (e.g., a project dashboard).
- **Goal:** Ensure cross-boundary collaboration.
- **Reflection:** Did alignment reduce friction? What connections need strengthening?

Day 5: Address Resistance

- **Action:** Identify one source of team resistance to the goal. Host a feedback session to listen and address concerns with empathy.
- **Goal:** Build buy-in and momentum.
- **Reflection:** Did listening reduce resistance? How can you sustain engagement?

Day 6: Celebrate Progress

- **Action:** Recognize one team member's contribution to the goal publicly (e.g., in a meeting or email) to boost morale.
- **Goal:** Sustain motivation.
- **Reflection:** Did recognition boost enthusiasm? How can you celebrate more effectively?

Day 7: Reflect and Adjust

- **Action:** Schedule 30 minutes to journal one lesson from the week and set a goal to improve vision translation (e.g., clearer communication, better alignment).

- **Goal:** Consolidate learning and plan growth.
- **Reflection:** How did this week's actions enhance your impact? What's your next step?

This plan empowers middle leaders to translate vision effectively, driving alignment and impact.

Conclusion

Middle leaders are indispensable as vision carriers and translators. They transform abstract strategies into actionable, meaningful work that drives organizational success by emphasizing the "why," clarifying goals, connecting tasks to mission, and defining success. Middle leaders create alignment, engagement, and purpose.

Beyond implementation, middle leaders influence culture, nurture talent, and maintain momentum through challenges. Their ability to communicate, adapt, and inspire ensures that vision is not just aspirational but achievable.

Organizations that recognize and empower middle leaders in this role position themselves for sustained success, innovation, and growth. Middle leadership is both a responsibility and a privilege. Operating in this space requires skill, wisdom, and intentionality; however, those who fully embrace it become the heartbeat of their organizations, ensuring that vision, strategy, and human effort converge to produce a lasting, meaningful impact.

"Trust is the glue of life. It's the most essential ingredient in effective communication. It's the foundational principle that holds all relationships."
— Stephen R. Covey

"A truthful witness saves lives, but a false witness is deceitful."
— Proverbs 14:25

Chapter 5:
Building Trust and Relationships

Chapter 4 explored the critical role of effective communication in middle leadership, emphasizing how clear, empathetic, and strategic interactions drive alignment and engagement.

As middle leaders master the art of conveying vision and fostering dialogue, they lay the groundwork for the next essential pillar of leadership: trust. Without trust, even the most eloquent communication falls flat, as credibility and connection are what truly bring strategies to life.

Chapter 5, "Building Trust and Relationships," delves into this foundational element, offering practical insights and a structured action plan to help middle leaders cultivate trust across all levels of the organization, ensuring their influence is both impactful and enduring.

Introduction: The Foundation of Leadership

Trust is the lifeblood of middle leadership. With trust, middle leaders can swiftly transform positional authority into genuine influence. Allowing them to navigate the complexities of their role. Unlike senior leaders who wield formal power, middle leaders thrive on earned credibility, forged through authentic relationships. Their ability to inspire confidence, foster collaboration, and bridge organizational divides determines whether strategies succeed or falter.

In today's workplace, trust is a non-negotiable skill. Research from the Center for Creative Leadership reveals that employees who trust their managers are nearly twice as likely to be engaged, productive, and loyal. Conversely, a lack of trust breeds disengagement, turnover, and misalignment, undermining organizational goals. For middle leaders, building trust is a strategic imperative, not just a relational nicety. Their influence hinges on the strength of relationships they nurture, upward with senior leadership, downward with their teams, and laterally with peers.

Leadership, at its core, is relational. Strategies and visions provide direction, but relationships are the conduits through which they flow. Trust is the foundation that makes middle leadership effective, sustainable, and transformative.

Building Trust in Every Direction

Middle leaders operate at the nexus of organizational dynamics, acting as translators of vision, connectors of people, and mediators of conflict. To succeed, they must cultivate trust in three directions: upward, downward, and laterally.

1. Building Upward Trust

Trust with senior leaders is rooted in reliability and competence. Executives rely on middle leaders to execute strategies, anticipate challenges, and align with organizational goals. This requires more than following orders; it demands translating high-level vision into actionable plans while offering honest, constructive feedback, making sure they do not hurt any employee.

Consider a project manager who consistently delivers on deadlines and proactively communicates risks. Their track record earns them credibility, making senior leaders more receptive to their insights. This shifts the middle leader's role from executor to trusted advisor. Upward trust is built through consistent delivery, discretion with sensitive information, and alignment with the organization's mission, even when offering critical feedback.

2. Building Downward Trust

Trust with direct reports hinges on integrity, empathy, and consistency. Team members observe whether their leader keeps promises, communicates transparently, and genuinely cares about their well-being. A leader who balances accountability with flexibility, such as offering hybrid work options while maintaining performance standards, demonstrates trust in their team, fostering loyalty and discretionary effort.

For example, a team leader who acknowledges achievements, addresses concerns promptly, and applies discipline fairly creates a culture of mutual respect. Employees feel valued, which drives engagement and reduces turnover. Downward trust thrives when leaders show that accountability and care are complementary, not contradictory.

3. Building Lateral Trust

Lateral trust, often overlooked, is critical for cross-functional collaboration. Middle leaders must align competing priorities across departments to achieve shared goals. By listening actively, acknowledging contributions, and modeling respect, they reduce silos and foster innovation.

Imagine a middle leader coordinating a product launch across marketing, engineering, and operations. By valuing each team's perspective and facilitating open dialogue, they build trust that streamlines problem-solving and creates collective ownership. Without lateral trust, collaboration becomes transactional; with it, organizations gain agility and resilience.

A Biblical Example: Jonathan and David

The relationship between Jonathan and David (**1 Samuel 18–20**) offers a timeless lesson in trust. As heir to King Saul's throne, Jonathan could have viewed David as a rival. Instead, he chose loyalty, supporting David at significant personal cost. His integrity, humility, and sacrifice forged a bond that endured intense pressure.

For middle leaders, Jonathan's example underscores that trust requires prioritizing the organization's success over personal ambition. By acting with integrity and humility, leaders build relationships that withstand challenges and create lasting impact.

A Modern Example: Google's Project Aristotle

Google's Project Aristotle study found that psychological safety—the belief that one can speak up, take risks, or admit mistakes without fear— is the most significant predictor of team success. Middle leaders shape this environment by encouraging open dialogue, modeling vulnerability, and valuing diverse perspectives.

For instance, a software team manager who welcomes bold ideas, even if some fail, fosters innovation. By admitting their own missteps and framing failures as learning opportunities, they create a culture where team members feel safe to contribute fully. This psychological safety drives collaboration, creativity, and resilience.

The Role of Emotional Intelligence in Trust-Building

Emotional intelligence (EQ) is the backbone of trust. Middle leaders with high EQ navigate relational complexities, resolve conflicts, and inspire others effectively. Key components include:

- **Self-Awareness:** Understanding how one's actions and tone impact others allows leaders to adjust and avoid eroding trust unintentionally.

- **Self-Regulation:** Staying composed under pressure signals reliability, reassuring teams during uncertainty.

- **Empathy:** Validating others' perspectives builds relational depth, showing genuine care.

- **Social Skills:** Effective communication, conflict resolution, and persuasion strengthen trust networks.

By honing EQ, middle leaders create environments where people feel understood, respected, and motivated.

Practical Strategies for Building Trust

Trust requires intentional, consistent habits. Middle leaders can adopt these practices:

- **Active Listening:** Give full attention, ask clarifying questions, and reflect understanding to show respect.

- **Transparency:** Explain the "why" behind decisions to reduce uncertainty and build confidence.

- **Consistency:** Follow through on commitments and apply standards fairly to establish reliability.

- **Recognition:** Celebrate achievements, both big and small, to reinforce a culture of appreciation.

- **Support Risk-Taking:** Encourage experimentation and treat mistakes as growth opportunities.

- **Regular Check-Ins:** Maintain ongoing dialogue to build rapport and address concerns proactively.

These habits, though simple, create ripple effects that strengthen organizational trust.

Weekly Action Plan for Building Trust

To operationalize trust-building, middle leaders can follow this structured weekly plan, designed to reinforce habits and track progress over time. This plan aligns with the strategies above and can be adapted to specific team dynamics.

Week 1: Establish a Trust Baseline

- **Objective**: Assess current trust levels and set a foundation.
- **Actions**:
  - Conduct one-on-one check-ins with 2–3 team members to understand their concerns and aspirations.
  - Identify one opportunity to demonstrate reliability to senior leaders (e.g., deliver a report early).
  - Reach out to a peer in another department to discuss a shared goal or challenge.
- **Reflection**: At week's end, journal about feedback received and areas where trust feels strong or weak.

Week 2: Strengthen Downward Trust

- **Objective**: Build credibility and connection with direct reports.
- **Actions**:
  - Recognize one team member's contribution publicly (e.g., in a team meeting or email).
  - Practice active listening in a team discussion, summarizing others' points before responding.

o Share the reasoning behind a recent decision to increase transparency.

- **Reflection**: Note how team members respond to recognition and transparency. Are they more engaged?

Week 3: Enhance Upward Trust

- **Objective**: Deepen credibility with senior leadership.
- **Actions**:
  o Prepare a concise update for a senior leader, highlighting progress and one actionable insight.
  o Anticipate a potential challenge in your team's work and propose a solution proactively.
  o Follow through on a commitment made to a senior leader, ensuring timely delivery.
- **Reflection**: Assess whether senior leaders respond positively to your proactive approach.

Week 4: Foster Lateral Trust

- **Objective**: Build stronger cross-functional relationships.
- **Actions**:
  o Schedule a brief meeting with a peer in another department to align on a shared priority.
  o Acknowledge a contribution from another team during a cross-functional meeting.
  o Offer support to a peer facing a challenge, such as sharing a resource or insight.
- **Reflection**: Evaluate whether collaboration with peers feels smoother or more productive.

Ongoing (Weeks 5–8 and Beyond):

- **Objective**: Sustain and deepen trust across all directions.
- **Actions**:

o Rotate focus weekly between upward, downward, and lateral trust-building activities.

o Conduct a monthly team survey to gauge trust and psychological safety levels.

o Dedicate 15 minutes weekly to self-reflection on EQ, noting areas for growth (e.g., empathy, self-regulation).

o Celebrate a team or cross-departmental win to reinforce collective trust.

- **Reflection**: Track progress in a journal, noting shifts in team morale, collaboration, or senior leader confidence.

This action plan ensures trust-building becomes a deliberate, measurable practice, embedded in daily leadership.

Overcoming Common Trust-Building Challenges

Building trust isn't without obstacles. Middle leaders may face:

- **Time Constraints**: Juggling operational demands can limit relationship-building time. Solution: Prioritize brief, high-impact interactions, like 10-minute check-ins or quick recognition emails.

- **Conflict or Misalignment**: Differing priorities across teams can erode trust. Solution: Use active listening and empathy to find common ground and align goals.

- **Skepticism from Teams**: Past leadership failures may make employees wary. Solution: Model consistency and transparency to rebuild confidence over time.

- **Cultural Differences**: Diverse teams may have varying expectations of trust. Solution: Invest in understanding cultural nuances and adapting communication styles.

By anticipating these challenges and addressing them proactively, middle leaders can maintain trust even in complex environments.

The Ripple Effect of Trust

Trust amplifies influence. A middle leader who embodies integrity and care doesn't just strengthen their team; they shape the organization's culture. Trust reduces friction, accelerates decision-making, and cultivates unity in the organization. Conversely, its absence creates silos, suspicion, and inefficiency.

When leaders prioritize trust, they empower others to contribute fully. Teams become more collaborative, innovative, and resilient, driving organizational success. Trust also enhances a leader's reputation, making them a go-to figure for advice and collaboration across the organization.

Case Study: Turning Around a Disengaged Team

Consider Sarah, a middle leader in a healthcare organization tasked with leading a disengaged clinical team. Turnover was high, and collaboration with other departments was strained. Sarah implemented a trust-building strategy:

- **Downward Trust:** She held weekly check-ins, listened to concerns, and recognized small wins, like a nurse's creative scheduling solution.

- **Upward Trust:** She provided concise, data-driven updates to senior leaders, highlighting her team's progress and challenges.

- **Lateral Trust:** She met regularly with the operations team to align on shared goals, reducing scheduling conflicts.

- **EQ Focus:** Sarah practiced self-regulation during tense meetings, modeling calm and encouraging open dialogue.

Within six months, turnover dropped by **20%**, team morale improved, and cross-departmental collaboration streamlined patient care. Sarah's trust-building efforts created a ripple effect, transforming her team and influencing the broader organization.

Trust in Crisis: A Stress Test

Trust is most critical during crises. When challenges arise, be it a missed deadline, a budget cut, or a public relations issue, trust determines how teams respond. A leader who has built strong relationships can rally support, maintain morale, and navigate uncertainty. Without trust, crises amplify division and dysfunction.

For example, during a supply chain disruption, a trusted middle leader can coordinate with peers, reassure their team, and provide clear updates to senior leaders. Their credibility helps ensure alignment and resilience, turning challenges into opportunities for growth.

Sustaining Trust Over Time

Trust is not a one-time achievement; it requires ongoing effort. Middle leaders must:

- **Stay Consistent:** Regularly deliver on promises to maintain credibility.

- **Adapt to Change:** As teams or priorities shift, adjust trust-building strategies to stay relevant.

- **Seek Feedback:** Use surveys or one-on-ones to gauge trust levels and identify blind spots.

- **Model Vulnerability:** Share appropriate personal challenges or mistakes to humanize leadership and encourage openness.

By embedding trust into their daily rhythm, middle leaders ensure it remains a cornerstone of their influence.

Conclusion: Trust as a Legacy

Trust is more than a leadership tool; it's a legacy. Middle leaders who invest in building trust upward, downward, and laterally become catalysts for organizational health. They bridge divides, inspire loyalty, and drive results that outlast their tenure.

Biblical examples like Jonathan and David and modern insights like Google's Project Aristotle highlight the timeless principles of trust: integrity, empathy, and consistency.

By benefiting from emotional intelligence and practical strategies, middle leaders transform abstract ideals into tangible practices that elevate teams and organizations.

Ultimately, trust is the currency of influence. Middle leaders who prioritize it don't just achieve goals; they shape cultures, empower people, and leave a lasting impact. Their legacy lies not in their title but in the relationships they build and the trust they inspire.

Chapter 6:
Navigating Organizational Politics

Chapter 5 highlighted how trust and relationships form the bedrock of middle leadership, allowing influence through integrity, empathy, and consistent action. Yet, even in environments rich with trust, organizational realities introduce complexities like competing interests and power dynamics that can challenge these bonds. Navigating these waters requires political savvy, using influence ethically to advance goals without compromising values.

Chapter 6, "Navigating Organizational Politics," equips middle leaders with the wisdom and strategies to engage these dynamics constructively, turning potential obstacles into opportunities for alignment and progress.

Introduction: The Reality of Politics at Work

Organizational politics is an inevitable aspect of leadership, particularly for middle leaders who are sandwiched between executive directives and team execution.

It includes the interplay of influence, relationships, and power to allocate resources, resolve conflicts, and drive initiatives. The work politics are often vilified as manipulative, but they can instead be a force for ethical advancement when approached with skill and integrity.

Middle leaders encounter politics daily through competing priorities and scarce resources. Mastering it enhances influence, secures support, and boosts job satisfaction, as supported by research from Ferris and colleagues (**2005**). Ignoring it risks isolation and stalled progress. Politics, then, is a competency that aligns personal and organizational goals ethically.

Defining Organizational Politics

Organizational politics encompasses the use of power and influence to achieve outcomes in group settings. It emerges from scarce resources, unclear goals, or conflicting interests, manifesting in both formal (hierarchical) and informal (relational) structures.

Key triggers include resource competition, strategic ambiguity, and stakeholder misalignment. Elements involve ethical persuasion, negotiation, and conflict mediation.

For middle leaders, engagement means recognizing these dynamics and leveraging them to foster collaboration, not division. Ethical politics aligns influence with shared values, enhancing overall effectiveness.

Biblical Principles for Political Wisdom

Scripture provides timeless guidance for handling influence and conflict:

- Proverbs 15:1 emphasizes gentle responses to defuse anger, promoting productive dialogue.

- Matthew 10:16 advises being "wise as serpents and innocent as doves," blending discernment with purity.

- Romans 12:17–21 urges overcoming evil with good, focusing on reconciliation over retaliation.

These principles anchor middle leaders in character amid political navigation, ensuring actions reflect integrity and build rather than erode relationships.

Formal and Informal Power Structures

Understanding power sources is essential for all middle leaders. Formal power stems from titles and hierarchies, dictating decision flows and resource allocation. Middle leaders use this for efficient escalation and boundary respect.

Informal power arises from expertise, networks, and trust, often outweighing titles in real influence. A respected advisor without a senior role can sway outcomes through credibility. Middle leaders who map both structures avoid pitfalls and uncover collaboration avenues, amplifying their impact beyond positional limits.

Ethical Influence

Sustainable influence demands ethics. Shortcuts like manipulation erode trust; ethical approaches build it. Strategies include clear communication of rationales, stakeholder motivation analysis, coalition-building on shared objectives, and transparent decisions.

For instance, in a budget dispute, a middle leader might facilitate discussions, identify overlaps, and propose value-aligned compromises. This resolves issues while strengthening ties, demonstrating that ethical influence advances collective success.

Conflict Resolution: Turning Tension into Opportunity

Conflict signals diverse perspectives, not failure. Effective resolution prevents escalation and harnesses differences for innovation. Steps involve early identification, active listening, issue-personality separation, fair negotiation, and agreement follow-up.

In practice, mediating a team rift over priorities by reframing it around organizational mission turns tension into aligned effort. Wise handling positions middle leaders as impartial facilitators, enhancing their credibility.

Real-Life Example: PepsiCo

At PepsiCo, a mid-level manager navigated competitive idea pitches by aligning proposals with company goals, building peer credibility through competence and honesty. Without favoritism, she gained executive buy-in, advancing her career and initiatives. This underscores ethical politics as a pathway to organizational contribution, not personal gain.

Positive and Negative Examples of Politics in Action

Negative: A leader undermines a peer via rumors for promotion, eroding morale and trust long-term.

Positive: Mediating inter-departmental disputes by emphasizing mutual benefits and fostering ongoing partnerships.

These illustrate the choice's impact: destructive politics fragments, ethical unites.

Research Insights: Why Political Skill Matters

Ferris et al. (**2005**) link political skill to career success, influence, and results. Skilled leaders read cues, network effectively, and drive outcomes ethically, while boosting engagement. This strategy helps them to transform awareness into service, aligning power flows for the broader good.

Practical Strategies for Middle Leaders

- **Map the Landscape:** Chart stakeholders, priorities, and power sources.
- **Build Credibility:** Deliver consistently to earn trust.
- **Communicate Strategically:** Adapt messages to audiences.
- **Leverage Coalitions:** Ally on common goals.
- **Stay Ethical:** Prioritize integrity over shortcuts.
- **Manage Conflict:** Proactively mediate tensions.

These tools empower middle leaders to influence positively.

Weekly Action Plan for Navigating Politics

This progressive plan helps middle leaders develop political acumen deliberately, with weekly focuses building cumulative skills. Track via a journal, adjusting based on reflections.

Week 1: Assess and Map the Landscape

- **Objective**: Gain awareness of formal and informal dynamics.
- **Actions**:
    - List key stakeholders, their roles, priorities, and influence sources.
    - Observe one meeting for power cues (e.g., who speaks last, alliances).

- o Identify one ethical influence opportunity, like sharing credit.
- **Reflection**: What surprised you about informal networks? How can integrity guide engagement?

Week 2: Build Ethical Influence Foundations

- **Objective**: Practice transparent communication and coalition-building.
- **Actions**:
  - o Communicate a decision's rationale to your team or peers clearly.
  - o Reach out to one stakeholder to understand their motivations.
  - o Propose a shared-goal idea in a cross-team discussion.
- **Reflection**: Did transparency reduce resistance? Note shifts in receptivity.

Week 3: Enhance Conflict Resolution Skills

- **Objective**: Address tensions proactively.
- **Actions**:
  - o Identify a brewing conflict and facilitate a listening session.
  - o Use gentle responses (per Proverbs 15:1) in a heated exchange.
  - o Document a resolution agreement and follow up mid-week.
- **Reflection**: How did ethical handling affect relationships? What wisdom was needed?

Week 4: Leverage Networks and Feedback

- **Objective**: Strengthen alliances and self-assess.

- **Actions**:
  - o Build one new coalition by offering help to a peer.
  - o Seek feedback from a trusted colleague on your political navigation.
  - o Apply biblical principles in a challenging interaction (e.g., reconciliation focus).
- **Reflection**: Evaluate alliance impacts and areas for ethical growth.

Ongoing (Weeks 5–8 and beyond):

- **Objective**: Integrate and sustain skills.
- **Actions**:
  - o Rotate strategies weekly (mapping, influencing, resolving).
  - o Conduct monthly stakeholder check-ins to monitor dynamics.
  - o Review research insights or scripture for inspiration.
  - o Celebrate an ethical win, like successful mediation, with involved parties.
- **Reflection**: Track career influence growth and organizational alignment improvements.

This plan embeds political skill into routines, ensuring ethical mastery over time.

Overcoming Common Political Pitfalls

Challenges abound: Misreading cues leads to blunders, which can be countered by observing patterns. Ethical dilemmas tempt shortcuts; recommit to values via mentorship. Over-engagement risks burnout; balance with boundaries. Cultural variances affect perceptions; adapt inclusively. Proactive strategies mitigate these, preserving integrity.

Case Study: Tech Firm Turnaround

In a tech company, middle leader Alex faced siloed departments blocking creativity. Mapping informal influencers, he built coalitions ethically, mediated conflicts with active listening, and aligned pitches to executive priorities. Within quarters, project approvals rose **30%**, collaboration improved, and his influence expanded, proving that skilled navigation drives results.

Politics in Times of Change

During mergers or restructurings, politics intensifies. Ethical leaders shine by communicating transparently, reconciling interests, and using discernment. This maintains stability, turns ambiguity into unity, and positions them as anchors.

The Long-Term Impact of Ethical Navigation

Mastered ethically, politics enhances resilience and culture. Leaders foster inclusive environments, model wisdom, and advance missions. Over time, it yields promotions, stronger networks, and organizational health.

Sustaining Political Wisdom

Ongoing development involves:

- Regular reflection on interactions.
- Seeking diverse perspectives.
- Aligning actions with principles.
- Mentoring others in ethical influence.

This ensures politics serves, not subverts, the leadership's purpose.

Conclusion: Politics as a Leadership Competency

Navigating politics is integral to middle leadership, blending power awareness with ethical action. Biblical wisdom and research affirm that integrity-amplified skill propels progress. Middle leaders who engage thus not only safeguard credibility but also cultivate collaborative cultures, transforming politics into a unifying force for enduring success.

"Before you are a leader, success is all about growing yourself. When you become a leader, success is all about growing others."

— Jack Welch

"Iron sharpens iron, and one person sharpens another."

— Proverbs 27:17

Chapter 7:
Driving Change from the Middle

Chapter 6 provided middle leaders with the tools to navigate organizational politics ethically, transforming power dynamics into pathways for collaboration and progress. Yet, even the most adept political navigation serves a greater purpose: enabling transformative action. As organizations evolve, middle leaders must not only maneuver within existing structures but also initiate shifts that align with emerging needs.

Chapter 7, "Driving Change from the Middle," empowers leaders to become agents of innovation, drawing on insights like Jack Welch's emphasis on growing others and the biblical truth that "iron sharpens iron," to guide teams through transformation with purpose and resilience.

Introduction

Middle leaders hold a pivotal role in organizational ecosystems, bridging the gap between strategic vision and frontline execution. Their proximity to daily operations reveals inefficiencies, while their access to senior insights informs broader goals. This vantage point makes them ideal change agents, catalysts who turn observations into actionable transformations.

Effective change leadership demands courage to disrupt norms, creativity for solutions, and resilience amid resistance. Without formal executive authority, middle leaders rely on influence, empathy, and strategy. In dynamic environments shaped by technological advances and shifting markets, mastering change is vital for personal and organizational thriving.

Understanding the Role of a Change Agent

Change agents go beyond implementation; they ignite and sustain transformation. They foresee obstacles, motivate stakeholders, and adapt strategies to ensure lasting impact. Core responsibilities include:

- **Spotting Opportunities for Improvement:** Vigilant observation of processes and dynamics uncovers hidden inefficiencies. For instance, a retail manager might identify stock discrepancies caused by outdated inventory systems, proposing digital upgrades to enhance accuracy and reduce waste.

- **Championing Innovation:** With compelling narratives backed by data, change agents rally support. They demonstrate value through pilots or stories, making abstract ideas tangible.

- **Building Coalitions:** Success hinges on collective buy-in. Engaging diverse stakeholders fosters ownership and reduces silos.

- **Guiding Adaptation:** Providing training and emotional support helps teams navigate discomfort, building skills for new realities.

- **Sustaining Momentum:** Celebrating milestones and monitoring progress keeps energy high, preventing initiative fatigue.

Key Strategies for Driving Change

Identifying Areas for Improvement

Change starts with insight and facts. Middle leaders collect data via surveys, observations, and metrics to pinpoint high-impact issues. Focusing on alignment with organizational priorities ensures efforts yield significant returns.

Case Study: In a logistics firm, a supervisor analyzed delivery delays, tracing them to inefficient routing. Implementing GPS-optimized software reduced transit times by **15%,** boosting customer satisfaction.

Building Support and Overcoming Resistance

Resistance stems from uncertainty or loss aversion. Address it with empathy: articulate benefits, involve influencers, and adapt based on feedback.

- Tactics:
- Link changes to personal and team gains.
- Use peer advocates to demonstrate success.
- Host forums for open dialogue.

Case Study: Introducing remote work in a traditional firm met skepticism. The leader shared success stories from pilots, addressed concerns like productivity tracking and phased implementation, leading to higher retention.

Pilot Programs and Scaling Initiatives

Testing small mitigates risks. Pilots gather real-world data, refine approaches, and build evidence for broader adoption.

Example: A nonprofit tested a new donor management tool in one branch. Adjustments based on user input ensured seamless organization-wide rollout, increasing fundraising efficiency.

Biblical Principles for Change Leadership

Scripture offers guidance for transformative leadership:

- Nehemiah 4:6 highlights unity: Collaborative effort rebuilds what's broken.
- Isaiah 43:19 encourages embracing novelty: God's renewal inspires innovation.
- Philippians 3:13-14 stresses perseverance: Focus forward amid challenges.

These principles frame change as a communal, faith-driven journey, emphasizing people over processes.

Common Challenges for Change Agents

- **Competing Priorities:** Balancing daily tasks with initiatives can be overwhelming.
- **Resistance:** Fear or inertia hinders adoption.
- **Limited Authority:** Influence must substitute for power.
- **Organizational Politics:** Agendas may conflict.
- **Resource Constraints:** Scarcity limits scope.
- **Sustaining Momentum:** Enthusiasm wanes without reinforcement.

- **Emotional Pressure:** Managing expectations from above and below strains leaders.
- **Cultural Barriers:** Norms resist upheaval.

Strategies to Overcome Challenges

- **Prioritize Strategically:** Tackle high-ROI changes first. Example: A tech lead focused on core software updates before peripherals, avoiding overload.
- **Engage Stakeholders Early:** Involve key players for input. Example: Union consultations smoothed manufacturing process changes.
- **Leverage Informal Influence:** Build trust networks. Example: Cross-team lunches fostered alliances in a marketing overhaul.
- **Communicate Transparently:** Regular updates build trust. Example: Bi-weekly newsletters during a CRM transition kept teams informed.
- **Support Well-Being:** Offer resources like workshops. Example: Stress management sessions aided educators during curriculum shifts.
- **Celebrate Wins:** Recognize progress. Example: Awards for safety milestones motivated hospital staff.
- **Adapt to Culture:** Customize approaches. Example: Region-specific policies enhanced global policy acceptance.

Emotional Intelligence in Driving Change

EI underpins successful transitions. Self-aware leaders manage stress; empathetic ones validate fears; socially skilled ones persuade effectively. Research from the Consortium for Research on Emotional Intelligence links high EI to better change outcomes, reducing turnover and boosting engagement.

Leaders cultivate EI by reflecting on reactions, practicing active listening, and seeking feedback, ensuring human elements drive sustainable change.

Step-by-Step Guide to Drive Change

This guide provides a structured approach for middle leaders to initiate and lead transformation effectively.

- **Assess the Current State:** Gather data on processes, performance, and pain points. Use surveys, interviews, and metrics to identify gaps. Example: Analyze workflow bottlenecks via time-tracking tools.

- **Define the Vision and Goals:** Articulate a clear, compelling future state aligned with organizational objectives. Set SMART goals (Specific, Measurable, Achievable, Relevant, Time-bound). Involve stakeholders for buy-in.

- **Build a Coalition:** Identify allies, such as influencers, peers, and supporters. Form a cross-functional team to share ownership and diverse perspectives.

- **Develop a Plan:** Outline steps, timelines, resources, and responsibilities. Include risk assessments and contingency measures. Use tools like Gantt charts for visualization.

- **Communicate Effectively:** Share the "why," "what," and "how" transparently. Tailor messages to audiences—data for executives, benefits for teams.

- **Implement in Phases:** Start with pilots to test and refine. Monitor progress with KPIs and adjust as needed.

- **Address Resistance:** Listen to concerns, provide training, and demonstrate quick wins to build momentum.

- **Sustain and Evaluate:** Celebrate achievements, embed changes into culture, and review outcomes. Conduct post-implementation audits for continuous improvement.

Following this guide ensures methodical, inclusive change, minimizing disruptions while maximizing impact.

Weekly Action Plan for Driving Change

Embed change leadership into routines with this plan, focusing on progressive skill-building.

Week 1: Assessment and Visioning

- **Objective**: Identify opportunities and clarify goals.
- **Actions**:
    - Conduct three feedback sessions with team members on current challenges.
    - Draft a vision statement for one potential change initiative.
    - Map stakeholders and their influence levels.
- **Reflection**: What insights emerged? How does the vision align with organizational priorities?

Week 2: Coalition Building

- **Objective**: Secure support networks.
- **Actions**:
    - Meet with two potential allies to discuss the initiative.
    - Share preliminary data highlighting improvement needs.
    - Address one anticipated resistance point proactively.
- **Reflection**: How did engagements build buy-in? Note any adjustments needed.

Week 3: Planning and Communication

- **Objective**: Create and convey the roadmap.
- **Actions**:
    - Outline a detailed plan with timelines and resources.
    - Communicate the vision in a team meeting or email.
    - Practice empathetic responses to potential concerns.
- **Reflection**: Was communication clear? Gauge initial reactions.

Week 4: Implementation Kickoff

- **Objective**: Launch initial efforts.
- **Actions**:
    - Initiate a small pilot or first phase.
    - Track early metrics and celebrate a quick win.
    - Provide support resources, like training materials.
- **Reflection**: What worked well? Identify early hurdles.

Ongoing (Weeks 5–8 and beyond):

- **Objective**: Maintain momentum and adapt.
- **Actions**:
    - Rotate focuses (e.g., sustainment one week, evaluation next).
    - Hold bi-weekly check-ins with coalition members.
    - Review biblical principles for inspiration during setbacks.
    - Adjust plan based on feedback and results.
- **Reflection**: Track overall progress and personal growth in change leadership.

This plan turns abstract strategies into actionable habits.

Research Insights on Change Management

Studies from McKinsey indicate that successful transformations are 8 times more likely when leaders model behaviors and engage employees. Kotter's 8-step model reinforces the guide above, emphasizing urgency, coalitions, and institutionalization. These insights validate the human-centric approach for middle leaders.

Case Study: Retail Transformation

In a chain store, middle manager Lisa spotted declining sales due to outdated inventory. Following the step-by-step guide, she assessed data, built a team with buyers and staff, piloted AI forecasting in one store, communicated benefits, addressed tech fears with training, and scaled successes. Sales rose **20%,** proving methodical change drives results.

The Human Side of Change: Fostering Growth

Echoing Welch and Proverbs, change is about development. Middle leaders mentor during transitions, offering feedback and opportunities. This sharpens skills, boosts morale, and creates a culture of continuous improvement.

Navigating Change in Volatile Environments

In uncertain times, like economic shifts, adaptability is key. Leaders monitor external trends, pivot plans, and maintain open channels. Example: During supply chain disruptions, a logistics leader realigned routes dynamically, preserving operations.

Integrating Technology in Change Initiatives

Leverage tools like project software (e.g., Asana) or analytics platforms to streamline efforts. Ensure training to avoid alienation, turning tech into an enabler.

Measuring Success: Beyond Metrics

While KPIs matter, qualitative measures, like employee satisfaction surveys, capture the full impact. Balanced scorecards provide holistic views.

Ethical Considerations in Driving Change

Uphold integrity: Avoid coercive tactics, ensure equity, and align with values. Biblical principles guide ethical decisions, fostering trust.

Practical Exercises for Middle Leaders

- Stakeholder Mapping: Chart influences and strategies.
- Resistance Analysis: Brainstorm counters to objections.
- EI Reflection: Journal emotional responses in past changes.
- Coalition Building: Engage three allies with tailored pitches.
- Celebration Plan: Schedule recognitions for milestones.

Conclusion

Driving change from the middle blends challenge with opportunity. As bridges between vision and reality, middle leaders catalyze growth through empathy, strategy, and perseverance. Biblical truths, research, and examples affirm that human-focused, ethical approaches yield enduring transformations. By embracing this role, leaders not only achieve objectives but also sharpen others, leaving legacies of innovation and resilience.

"You must take personal responsibility. You cannot change the circumstances, the seasons, or the wind, but you can change yourself."

— Jim Rohn

"For God gave us a spirit not of fear but of power and love and self-control."

— 2 Timothy 1:7

Chapter 8:
Leading Yourself First

Chapter 7 equipped middle leaders with strategies to drive change, emphasizing their role in bridging vision and execution while growing others, as echoed in Jack Welch's wisdom and Proverbs' imagery of iron sharpening iron. Yet, to truly empower teams and sustain transformations, leaders must first master themselves, taking unwavering ownership of their actions, growth, and responses amid chaos.

As Jocko Willink and Leif Babin articulate in "Extreme Ownership," true leadership begins with assuming full responsibility for outcomes, no excuses, enabling decisive influence from the middle. Chapter 8, "Leading Yourself First," delves into this essential foundation, exploring self-leadership through emotional intelligence, discipline, and accountability to build resilience and credibility.

Introduction

Effective middle leadership depends on self-mastery. Remember, no one will teach you the insights; you have to work toward them yourself. Before guiding teams, navigating politics, or driving change, leaders must lead themselves intentionally. Self-leadership combines awareness, discipline, accountability, and growth, forming the foundation for influencing others. Without it, external efforts struggle due to personal inconsistencies or unchecked reactions.

Cultivating self-leadership boosts team performance, curbs burnout, and enhances organizational health, per research from Gallup and Harvard Business Review. It transforms middle leaders into authentic role models, equipped to handle pressures with poise and inspire confidence.

Defining Emotional Intelligence

Emotional intelligence (EI) is the capacity to recognize, understand, manage, and utilize emotions in oneself and others. Coined by psychologists Peter Salovey and John Mayer, and popularized by Daniel Goleman, EI encompasses perceiving emotional cues, reasoning with emotions, comprehending their implications, and regulating them for positive outcomes.

Goleman's framework outlines five components:

- **Self-Awareness:** Accurately gauging one's emotions, strengths, and impacts. It involves real-time recognition of feelings and their drivers.

- **Self-Regulation:** Controlling impulses and adapting responses. Disciplined leaders channel emotions constructively, maintaining ethics under stress.

- **Motivation:** Harnessing inner drive for goals beyond external rewards. It fuels optimism and commitment amid setbacks.

- **Empathy:** Sensing others' emotions and perspectives. It fosters inclusive decisions and supportive environments.

- **Social Skills:** Building rapport, communicating persuasively, and resolving conflicts. Proficient leaders influence collaboratively.

EI operates as a dynamic skill set, applicable in personal reflection and interpersonal dynamics, enabling nuanced navigation of human elements in leadership.

Why EI Surpasses Academic Intelligence in Leadership

Academic intelligence (IQ) measures cognitive abilities like logic, analysis, and knowledge retention, which are vital for technical tasks. However, in leadership, especially middle management, EI often proves more predictive of success. Goleman's research shows EI accounts for up to **90%** of what distinguishes top performers in senior roles, while IQ plateaus in contributions beyond entry-level expertise.

Reasons EI eclipses IQ:

- **Relational Demands:** Leadership involves people, not just problems. High IQ solves equations; high EI builds alliances, motivates diverse teams, and resolves emotional conflicts. Studies from the Center for Creative Leadership indicate **75%** of derailed careers stem from EI deficits like poor interpersonal skills, not intellectual shortcomings.

- **Adaptability in Uncertainty:** IQ excels in stable, data-driven scenarios; EI thrives in ambiguity. Middle leaders face volatile priorities; EI enables emotional resilience, empathetic adaptation, and intuitive decision-making where facts alone fall short.

- **Influence Without Authority:** Positional power is limited; EI amplifies persuasion. Empathetic, self-regulated leaders earn trust, inspiring voluntary followership over compliance.

- **Long-Term Impact:** IQ drives short-term task mastery; EI sustains cultures. Yale's research links high EI to reduced stress, higher engagement, and lower turnover—outcomes IQ can't directly influence.

- **Ethical Navigation:** Emotions underpin values; EI ensures decisions align with integrity, preventing IQ-driven opportunism that erodes trust.

Meta-analyses in the Journal of Organizational Behavior confirm EI correlates strongly with leadership effectiveness (r=0.30) than IQ (r=0.20). In essence, while IQ opens doors, EI keeps leaders thriving inside, fostering environments where intelligence is amplified through collaboration.

Example: A brilliant engineer (high IQ) struggles as a manager due to dismissive feedback and alienating teams. An EI-savvy peer, with average IQ, motivates through empathy, yielding better results.

The Importance of Emotional Intelligence in Self-Leadership

EI anchors self-leadership by enabling thoughtful responses over reactions. Self-aware leaders spot biases; regulated ones maintain composure; motivated ones persist. Empathy and social skills extend inward, aligning actions with values.

In practice: During crises, EI prevents escalation, preserving credibility. High-EI leaders report **20%** lower burnout per TalentSmart studies, modeling resilience for teams.

Self-Discipline: The Engine of Personal Leadership

Discipline enforces priorities amid distractions. For middle leaders, it means structured routines upholding commitments.

Applications:

- **Time Management:** Block focus periods, delegate low-value tasks.
- **Behavioral Consistency:** Uphold standards uniformly.
- **Goal Pursuit:** Break objectives into daily actions.

Tesla leaders exemplify this: Rigorous schedules and detail orientation drove innovation under pressure.

Biblical Tie: 1 Corinthians 9:27 calls for bodily discipline, mirroring leadership self-control.

Taking Ownership

Ownership entails full accountability, without excuses. It shifts mindsets from victimhood to empowerment, as in "Extreme Ownership."

Applications:

- **Proactive Solutions:** Tackle issues head-on.
- **Lesson Learning:** Debrief failures constructively.
- **Team Accountability:** Own collective results.

Example: A delayed project leader analyzes root causes, implements fixes, and communicates transparently, rebuilding trust.

Proverbs 4:23 guards the heart, linking inner accountability to outer efficacy.

The Process of Leading Yourself First

A structured roadmap integrates elements:

- **Self-Assessment:** Use journals or Myers-Briggs for insights. Track emotional patterns weekly.

- **Goal Setting:** Align personal KPIs with org vision; e.g., enhance EI via reading Goleman quarterly.
- **Prioritization:** The Eisenhower Matrix distinguishes urgent-important tasks.
- **Emotional Regulation:** Mindfulness apps; reframe stressors. Proverbs 16:32 praises the slow-to-anger.
- **Continuous Learning:** Podcasts, mentors; adapt from feedback. 2 Timothy 2:15 urges diligent preparation.
- **Accountability Checkpoints:** Bi-monthly reviews with peers.
- **Modeling Behaviors:** Consistent actions influence subtly.

Stress Management and Resilience Building

Resilience rebounds from adversity. Strategies:

- **Networks:** Seek support circles.
- **Reflection:** Journal for perspective.
- **Controllables Focus:** Ignore externals, act on internals.
- **Wins Celebration:** Boost dopamine sustainably.

Physical health amplifies: Exercise regulates mood per APA studies.

Practical Integration in Daily Leadership

Blend EI, discipline, ownership: Start days with planning (discipline), respond empathetically in meetings (EI), own outcomes in reviews. This synergy handles **80%** of leadership challenges emotionally, per Goleman.

Case Study: A middle manager in finance, overwhelmed by audits, used EI to regulate anxiety, disciplined prep, and owned process improvements, reducing errors by **30%** and earning a promotion.

Overcoming Common Self-Leadership Pitfalls

- **Procrastination:** Combat with micro-habits.
- **Emotional Hijacks:** Pause techniques like breathing.
- **Isolation:** Mandate feedback loops.

- **Stagnation:** Annual development plans.

Address via coaching; EI training yields **25%** performance gains (IE Business School).

Research Insights on Self-Leadership

Google's Project Oxygen found that self-aware, disciplined leaders correlate with team success. Carnegie Institute: **85%** of financial success from EI-like skills, **15%** technical.

Biblically, 2 Timothy 1:7 empowers with self-control, banishing fear.

Reflective Exercises

- **EI Audit:** Score Goleman components; target low areas.
- **Ownership Review:** List recent decisions; assess responsibility taken.
- **Discipline Log:** Track habits for 30 days.

Long-Term Benefits: A Compounded Legacy

Mastered self-leadership compounds: Resilient leaders foster innovative cultures, retain talent, and ascend naturally. It aligns with Rohn's change-yourself ethos, turning middles into multipliers.

Conclusion

Leading yourself first is non-negotiable alchemy, transmuting personal potential into organizational gold. Emotional intelligence, surpassing IQ in its relational depth and adaptive power, equips middle leaders to conquer inner turmoil and external storms alike, regulating responses, empathizing profoundly, and motivating unrelentingly.

Bolstered by discipline's unyielding engine and ownership's radical accountability, this self-mastery forges unbreakable resilience, as Jim Rohn and Scripture affirm: true power lies in changing oneself amid unchangeable winds.

In an era where IQ opens doors but EI builds empires, middle leaders who prioritize this inner work don't just survive, they thrive, inspiring legions and etching legacies of integrity. Embrace it fiercely, for in leading yourself, you unlock the ultimate leverage: a spirit of power, love, and self-control that reshapes worlds.

"The function of leadership is to produce more leaders, not more followers."

— Ralph Nader.

"Whoever wants to become great among you must be your servant."

— Matthew 20:26

Chapter 9:
Coaching and Mentoring from the Middle

Introduction

Middle leaders stand at the crucible of organizational potential, immersed in operational realities yet attuned to strategic horizons. This vantage empowers them to sculpt talent, ignite leadership sparks, and weave a culture of growth through coaching and mentoring, twin engines of transformation. Coaching honed skills and performance in targeted bursts; mentoring nurtures holistic potential over time. Together, they demand empathy, credibility, and a servant's heart, turning influence into legacy without needing titles or thrones.

In this role, middle leaders don't command; they catalyze. Their commitment to others' ascent elevates engagement, innovation, and succession, creating ripples that fortify the entire enterprise. Passionate self-discipline from within fuels this outward mission, ensuring every interaction sharpens souls and skills alike.

The Role of Mentorship Without Formal Authority

Mentoring thrives beyond hierarchy, rooted in voluntary trust and mutual elevation. Free from power imbalances, it blooms authentically, drawing mentees through inspiration rather than obligation.

Core Principles:

- **Build Trust:** Forge bonds with unwavering integrity, confidentiality as sacred, interest as genuine fire.
- **Listen First:** Absorb dreams and doubts before dispensing wisdom; true guidance starts in silence.
- **Ask, Don't Tell:** Provoke self-discovery with questions that unlock inner reserves.
- **Lead by Example:** Embody excellence, discipline in action, resilience in storms to imprint lasting patterns.

- **Provide Constructive Feedback**: Deliver truths wrapped in encouragement, targeting actions for growth, not egos.

Example: Mary Barra at General Motors mentored from mid-ranks, investing in peers' ingenuity without leverage. Her servant-leadership built alliances, sparked innovations, and propelled her to CEO, proving middle-ground mentorship forges empires.

Peer Coaching Strategies

Peer coaching democratizes development, erasing barriers for collaborative sharpening. It breeds accountability and shared triumphs, amplifying collective strength.

Steps to Mastery:

- **Set Clear Objectives:** Anchor sessions in precise outcomes, aligning growth with purpose.
- **Active Listening:** Immerse fully, clarify, reflect, unearth depths.
- **Goal Alignment:** Link personal strides to organizational quests.
- **Encourage Reflection**: Pose piercing questions: What hidden lessons lurk? How to leap forward?
- **Follow-Up:** Cement progress with rhythmic check-ins, fueling unrelenting momentum.

Example: In tech teams, project managers swap stakeholder war stories, refining techniques through mutual coaching, which boosts influence sans authority.

Practical Tip: Ignite peer circles monthly, dissecting victories and trials to stoke continuous evolution.

Fostering Leadership Growth in Your Team

Cultivating leaders is middle leadership's noblest charge, spotting embers and fanning them into flames. This builds benches of readiness, empowering all.

Strategies:

- **Identify Potential:** Scout for hunger, aptitude, and heart.
- **Assign Stretch Assignments:** Thrust into challenges that stretch sinews, building mettle.
- **Model Behaviors:** Live accountability, foresight, decisiveness, discipline incarnate.
- **Provide Resources:** Arm with training, tools, and networks.
- **Encourage Reflection:** Instill journals of insight, turning experiences into wisdom.

Example: A manufacturing manager coached a delegator-to-be on priorities and resolution, catapulting them to supervision in months, team efficiency soaring.

Research Insights

Studies show the dividends: Mentored talent boasts 20% higher retention (Gallup), accelerated promotions, and resilient mindsets. Peer coaching slashes silos, boosts problem-solving by 25% (Journal of Vocational Behavior, Allen et al., 2008). Investing here isn't optional—it's the multiplier of organizational vitality.

Biblical Foundations for Coaching and Mentoring

Scripture pulses with this call:

- 2 Timothy 2:2: Entrust truths to the faithful, chaining generations of teachers.
- Proverbs 27:17: Iron on iron, mutual sharpening through relational fire.
- Titus 2:3–5: Elders guide youth in character and skill, servant-hearted.

Middle leaders, as conduits, transmit not just knowledge but divine servitude, shaping eternities.

Practical Exercises: Building a Mentorship Roadmap

Craft your blueprint:

- Identify Mentees: Pinpoint potentials and needs.
- Define Goals: SMART benchmarks for transformation.
- Select Approach: Solo, peer, or group dynamics.
- Schedule Touchpoints: Rhythmic pulses of progress.
- Track Progress: Log milestones, adapt fiercely.
- Reflect and Adjust: Quarterly audits for peak impact.

Example: Tech manager's quarterly engineer sessions blended skills drills with reflections, yielding confident leaders in a year.

Coaching and Mentoring in Action

Scenario 1: Manager coaches presentation-shy rep via feedback loops, and soon, independent powerhouses emerge. Scenario 2: Hospital mentor empowers nurses in coordination, slashing errors amid soaring morale. Scenario 3: Cross-regional circles in corporates breed global innovations through shared wisdom.

Overcoming Common Challenges

Hurdles loom, time scarcity, resistance, boundary blurs. Conquer with:

- Prioritize Ruthlessly: Carve sacred slots, delegate to focus on souls.
- Build Receptivity: Start small, celebrate wins to melt defenses.
- Set Boundaries: Clear roles prevent burnout, preserve passion.
- Leverage Tech: Virtual tools for seamless connections.
- Self-Discipline Integration: Your inner forge ensures consistency, meditate on goals daily, and reflect nightly.

Weekly Action Plan for Coaching and Mentoring

Infuse discipline into development with this structured plan:

Week 1: Identify and Initiate

- **Objective:** Spot and connect.
- **Actions:** List 3 potentials; schedule initial chats. Prepare listening questions.
- **Reflection:** What sparks did you ignite? How does servanthood feel?

Week 2: Build Trust and Goals

- **Objective:** Deepen bonds, set visions.
- **Actions:** Share vulnerabilities; co-create SMART goals. Model discipline in follow-through.
- **Reflection:** Trust levels rising? Adjust for authenticity.

Week 3: Active Coaching Sessions

- **Objective:** Guide discovery.
- **Actions:** Hold peer or one-on-one; ask provocative questions. Assign micro-stretches.
- **Reflection:** Self-discoveries noted? Your empathy's impact?

Week 4: Feedback and Follow-Up

- **Objective:** Reinforce growth.
- **Actions:** Deliver constructive insights; celebrate progress. Plan next steps.
- **Reflection:** Momentum building? Discipline in consistency paying off?

Ongoing (Weeks 5+):

- **Objective:** Sustain chains.
- **Actions:** Monthly circles; track via journals. Rotate mentees, integrate biblical insights.

- **Reflection**: Leaders emerging? Your legacy unfolding.

This plan demands your self-discipline; honor it passionately for exponential returns.

The Passionate Imperative of Self-Discipline in Mentoring

Self-discipline isn't optional; it's the heartbeat! Without it, sessions falter, follow-ups fade. Channel your Chapter 9 fire: Rise early for prep, resist distractions, hold yourself accountable to mentees' dreams. As Nader implies, produce leaders through your unrelenting commitment— serving with Matthew's humility, sharpening with Proverbs' edge. This discipline transforms mentoring from duty to divine calling, birthing empires of empowered souls.

Advanced Techniques: Reverse Mentoring and Group Dynamics

Embrace reverse mentoring, juniors teach seniors digital savvy, fostering humility. Group cohorts amplify peer learning, cross-pollinating ideas. Discipline ensures facilitation excellence.

Measuring Impact: Metrics and Stories

Track promotions, engagement scores, and feedback loops. Anecdotes reveal hearts changed, quantify, and qualify for full glory.

Ethical Considerations: Inclusivity and Equity

Mentor diverse voices, shatter biases. Servant-leadership demands fairness, amplifying underrepresented potential.

Case Study: Google's Mentoring Revolution

Middle managers at Google paired with mentees via algorithms, focusing on growth mindsets. Results: 30% faster innovations, diverse leaders rising, discipline in matching and follow-through key.

Conclusion

Coaching and mentoring from the middle is leadership's ultimate act of multiplication, serving to elevate and discipline to endure. With research-backed power, biblical mandates, and real-world triumphs like Barra's, middle leaders forge not followers but fellow forgers of fate. Embrace this with passionate self-discipline; produce leaders who produce more, in an unending chain of greatness.

Your influence, humbly wielded, reshapes organizations, and Chapter 10 passionately championed coaching and mentoring as the forge where middle leaders, through servant-hearted discipline, multiply influence by sharpening others into leaders. Yet, in an era of digital acceleration, this development demands modern amplifiers to resolve conflicts, align visions, and sustain peace amid chaos. As Gandhi noted, true peace is coping mastery, and Jesus blessed peacemakers as God's children. Chapter 11, "Technology and Tools for Influence," equips middle leaders to wield tech as a strategic ally, enhancing communication, data-driven decisions, and networking while navigating its perils with biblical wisdom.

"Peace is not the absence of conflict, but the ability to cope with it."
— Mahatma Gandhi.

"Blessed are the peacemakers, for they shall be called children of God."
— Matthew 5:9

Chapter 10:
Technology and Tools for Influence

Introduction

In the digital age, middle leaders bridge strategy and execution amid a relentless pace and dispersion. Technology transcends convenience; it's a force multiplier for influence, enabling coordination, insight, and connection without full authority. Mastering tools like collaboration platforms and analytics empowers leaders to align teams, champion ideas, and build credibility.

Digital fluency amplifies emotional intelligence and mentoring efforts, fostering alignment in hybrid worlds. Ignoring it risks irrelevance; embracing it strategically elevates impact, turning middle positions into pivotal hubs of innovation and resolution.

The Importance of Using Technology as an Effective Tool

Technology empowers middle leaders to:

- **Extend Reach:** Influence beyond physical limits, connecting global teams instantly.

- **Enhance Decision-Making:** Data tools provide evidence, reducing bias and bolstering proposals.

- **Boost Efficiency:** Automate routines, freeing time for high-value coaching and strategy.

- **Foster Inclusivity:** Asynchronous tools ensure diverse voices contribute, promoting equity.

- **Build Resilience:** In crises, tech maintains continuity, coping with disruptions peacefully.

Research from McKinsey shows digitally adept leaders drive **20-30%** higher performance. For middle leaders, it's essential: Tools translate visions, resolve misalignments, and sustain momentum, making influence scalable and sustainable.

Benefits of Technology in Leadership

- **Improved Communication:** Real-time platforms reduce misunderstandings, accelerating alignment.

- **Data-Driven Insights:** Analytics uncover trends, justifying initiatives with facts, e.g., KPIs reveal bottlenecks, enabling proactive fixes.

- **Collaboration Across Boundaries:** Suites like Microsoft **365** enable seamless teamwork, boosting innovation by **25%** (Deloitte studies).

- **Personal Branding:** LinkedIn sharing positions leaders as experts, expanding networks.

- **Efficiency and Productivity:** Automation tools like Zapier streamline workflows, minimizing errors.

- **Employee Engagement:** Feedback apps gauge sentiment, allowing timely interventions for morale.

- **Cost-Effectiveness:** Cloud solutions scale without heavy infrastructure, aiding resource-strapped middles.

Overall, tech amplifies influence, fosters peace through better conflict resolution (e.g., tracked discussions prevent escalation), and multiplies mentoring reach via virtual sessions.

Risks of Technology in Leadership

- **Over-Reliance:** Tools can't replace empathy; digital fatigue erodes relationships.

- **Data Privacy and Security:** Breaches undermine trust; cyber incidents rose **600%** in pandemics (IBM).

- **Digital Divide:** Unequal access excludes team members, breeding resentment.

- **Misinformation Spread:** Rapid sharing amplifies errors or biases.

- **Burnout from Constant Connectivity:** Always-on culture blurs boundaries, spiking stress.
- **Inequity in Adoption:** Tech-savvy leaders advance, widening gaps.
- **Distraction and Reduced Focus:** Notifications fragment attention, hampering deep work.

Mitigate by setting boundaries, training equitably, and prioritizing human elements, ensuring tech serves are not supplants but peacemaking.

Communication Platforms and Collaboration Tools

Essentials:

- **Messaging:** Slack for quick resolves, reducing email overload.
- **Video:** Zoom builds rapport via cues, vital for remote influence.
- **Project Management:** Asana tracks tasks, visualizing progress.
- **Knowledge Bases:** Confluence centralizes wisdom, cutting redundancy.

Applications: Share updates transparently, solicit ideas in channels. Example: Dropbox managers aligned via shared docs, influencing without authority.

Using Data to Support Influence

Leverage KPIs in Tableau for visuals that persuade executives. Surveys via Forms gather input, turning data into stories. Predictive tools anticipate issues, positioning leaders as foresightful.

Example: A Retail manager used analytics to pivot services, improving scores, and data as an influence amplifier.

Digital Networking and Professional Branding

LinkedIn posts share insights, building alliances. Internal forums spark cross-departmental mentoring. Consistency key: Weekly contributions elevate visibility.

Biblical Principles Relating to Proper Use of Technology

Scripture guides ethical, wise tech stewardship:

- **Proverbs 18:15:** "The heart of the discerning acquires knowledge, for the ears of the wise seek it out." Use tools to gain wisdom, not superficial data, and discern truth amid digital noise.

- **Luke 14:28:** Cost-counting before building applies to implementations: Assess ROI, risks, and human impact before adopting AI or platforms.

- **Ecclesiastes 7:12:** Knowledge as protection, leverage analytics for defense against errors, but pair with moral discernment.

- **Colossians 3:23:** Work heartily as for the Lord, use tech with integrity, avoiding manipulation (e.g., deepfakes) or overwork.

- **Matthew 5:9:** Peacemakers are blessed, tech resolves conflicts via transparent logs, but fosters reconciliation, not division through anonymous forums.

- **1 Corinthians 10:23:** All things lawful but not beneficial, evaluate if social media distracts from relationships or spreads gossip.

Bible views tools neutrally: Fire warms or burns; tech connects or isolates. Proper use demands stewardship, prioritizing people (**Exodus 20:13-17**, ethics in data handling), humility (avoiding idolizing gadgets, per **Isaiah 44:9-20**), and Sabbath rest from screens for reflection.

Reflection: Like the tower builder, plan tech deployments prayerfully, ensuring they glorify God by serving others without harm.

Research Insights

Tech boosts influence: MIT studies show collaborative tools enhance knowledge flow, per Majchrzak et al. (2005). Risks like overload, noted in Harvard Business Review, balance is essential.

Case Study: Tech-Enabled Peacemaking

In a fractured multinational team, a middle leader deployed Teams for mediated dialogues and Power BI for neutral data views. Conflicts resolved via recorded sessions, trust rebuilt, project succeeded, echoing Gandhi's concept of peace.

Practical Tips and Integration

Audit tools quarterly; train inclusively. Blend with EI: Video for empathy reads. Weekly: Post insights, analyze one metric.

Weekly Action Plan for Tech Integration

Week 1: Audit and Select

- Assess current tools; research one new (e.g., Slack).
- Train team on basics.
- Reflection: Biblical cost-counted?

Week 2: Communication Focus

- Launch channel for feedback.
- Host video check-in.
- Reflection: Enhanced alignment?

Week 3: Data Dive

- Track KPI; visualize findings.
- Share recommendations.
- Reflection: Risks mitigated?

Week 4: Network Build

- Post on LinkedIn; engage internally.
- Evaluate privacy ethics.
- Reflection: Influence grown?

Ongoing: Monthly reviews, adapt with Proverbs wisdom, ensure tech serves peacemaking.

Overcoming Digital Pitfalls

Counter risks: Policies for off-hours, inclusive access trainings. Foster offline bonds to humanize.

Conclusion

Technology is a double-edged sword, magnifying influence when wielded wisely. Its benefits, connectivity, insights, and efficiency empower middle leaders to bridge divides, while risks like isolation demand vigilant stewardship. Biblical principles illuminate proper use: Discern knowledge, count costs, work ethically, and pursue peace, ensuring tools amplify God's call to servanthood.

In blending technology with human wisdom, middle leaders become digital peacemakers, resolving conflicts with heightened empathy and data-driven truth. Embrace this fusion wholeheartedly: not as masters over machines, but as stewards of influence, shaping organizations where innovation and integrity thrive under divine souls forever.

"It is not the strongest of the species that survive, nor the most intelligent, but the one most responsive to change."

— Charles Darwin.

"Do not be conformed to this world, but be transformed by the renewal of your mind."

— Romans 12:2

Chapter 11:
Cross-Cultural Leadership in the Middle

Chapter 10 harnessed technology as a peacemaking force, enabling middle leaders to bridge divides and foster harmony amid digital disruptions, guided by Gandhi's resilience and biblical calls to unity. Yet, in a world of accelerating globalization, actual influence demands adaptability not just to tools, but to the rich tapestry of human diversity, echoing Darwin's survival through responsiveness and the Romans' transformation of mind. Chapter 11, "Cross-Cultural Leadership in the Middle," empowers leaders to thrive in multicultural arenas, navigating sensitivities with empathy and wisdom to build inclusive, innovative teams that transcend borders and biases.

A Note on Integrating Darwin and Biblical Principles

The inclusion of Charles Darwin's quote alongside biblical doctrine may raise questions, given the perceived conflict between evolutionary theory and creationist views. Darwin's broader scientific observations on adaptation and responsiveness to environmental shifts offer valuable insights into leadership agility, independent of debates on origins. This book draws from diverse wisdom traditions, secular and sacred, to equip leaders practically, much like Proverbs integrates observations of the natural world (e.g., ants in **Proverbs 6:6**) without endorsing every philosophical underpinning. The biblical principle from **Romans 12:2** takes primacy, emphasizing spiritual and mental transformation over mere survival instincts. Here, Darwin's idea illustrates a universal truth: adaptability fosters effectiveness, while Scripture provides the ethical and redemptive foundation, renewing minds to align with God's inclusive design for humanity (**Galatians 3:28**). This synthesis encourages discernment, gleaning timeless principles without compromising faith.

Introduction

Globalization requires middle leaders to understand cross-cultural dynamics to bring together diverse teams. This skill encourages collaboration, sparks innovation, and achieves results. Positioned between strategy and execution, middle leaders must adjust to cultural differences and promote inclusion where everyone feels valued.

Embracing diversity challenges biases and enhances emotional intelligence. Leaders who ignore it risk alienation; those who harness it gain competitive edges. Biblical unity in **Galatians 3:28** inspires impartiality, urging leaders to model equity in daily interactions.

Understanding Cultural Differences

Culture influences values, communication, and behaviors. Recognizing these roots prevents misjudgments.

Key Areas:

- **Communication Styles:** Directness varies; adapt to avoid offense.
- **Decision-Making:** Balance consensus with hierarchy based on norms.
- **Authority Views:** Tailor motivation to cultural respect levels.
- **Time Perceptions:** Align expectations to reduce tensions.

Tip: Use team surveys for insights.

Example: A manager in a global project created subgroup discussions for collectivist members, ensuring inclusive input and better decisions.

Inclusive Communication

Clear, adaptive communication builds trust across cultures.

Strategies:

- **Active Listening**: Decode cues holistically.
- **Simplify Language:** Eliminate confusing elements.
- **Clarify Expectations:** Define terms explicitly.
- **Encourage Feedback:** Build safe channels.

Biblical Tie: Acts 10:34-35 promotes fairness; inclusive dialogue reflects this.

Exercise: Audit recent communications for cultural clarity; refine accordingly.

Building Diverse Teams

Diversity fuels creativity and resilience.

Actions:

- **Recruit Broadly:** Seek varied backgrounds.
- **Ensure Safety:** Promote open sharing.
- **Cross-Pollinate:** Mix experiences via rotations.
- **Model Inclusion:** Celebrate all contributions.

Example: Satya Nadella at Microsoft fosters growth mindsets, boosting global engagement through empathetic input.

Exercise: Assess team diversity; plan one inclusivity boost.

Research Insights

Culturally adept leadership yields higher trust, creativity, and performance (Rockstuhl et al., 2011). Inclusive firms excel financially, per McKinsey reports.

Adapting Leadership Styles

Flexibility meets diverse needs.

Approaches:

- **Style Shifts**: Toggle directive-participative.
- **Personalized Support**: Customize feedback.
- **Conflict Handling**: Resolve sensitively.

Biblical Insight: **1 Corinthians 9:22** advocates adaptation for impact, while holding values.

Challenges in Cross-Cultural Leadership

Hurdles include miscommunication, biases, resistance, and integration. Mitigate via training and feedback.

Example: A finance leader bridged analytical and relational styles through workshops, enhancing collaboration.

Navigating the Sensitivity of Cross-Cultural Leadership in Today's Environment

In 2025's volatile landscape marked by cancel culture, social media scrutiny, and polarized politics, cross-cultural leadership requires heightened vigilance. Missteps can amplify online, eroding trust or careers.

Key Sensitivities:

- **Cancel Culture Risks:** Public shaming for perceived insensitivities demands proactive education. Leaders must foster dialogue over judgment, using empathy to de-escalate.
- **Political Volatility:** Global events (e.g., elections, conflicts) influence teams. Maintain neutrality, focusing on shared goals to avoid division.
- **Social Climate:** Rising awareness of equity issues necessitates addressing microaggressions and biases head-on.

Strategies:

- **Build Awareness:** Regular DEI training; self-reflect on biases.
- **Promote Open Dialogue:** Safe spaces for discussing sensitivities without fear.
- **Leverage Technology Ethically:** Use tools for inclusive virtual interactions, monitoring for equitable participation.
- **Respond to Incidents:** Address conflicts transparently, turning them into learning opportunities.
- **Stay Informed:** Follow global trends via reputable sources to anticipate impacts.

Biblical Guidance: **Romans 12:18** urges living peaceably; apply by renewing minds against worldly conformity, embracing transformation through understanding.

Example: Amid the 2024 U.S. elections' ripple effects, a middle leader in a multinational firm hosted neutral forums on work impacts, strengthening unity.

This navigation builds resilience, turning volatility into growth catalysts.

Exercises for Developing Cross-Cultural Leadership

- **Awareness Audit:** Catalog team cultures; note differences.
- **Feedback Practice:** Solicit style input; adapt.
- **Cross-Cultural Mentorship:** Pair diverse members.
- **Journaling:** Log interactions monthly.

Integrating Cross-Cultural Leadership Into Middle Leadership

Weave into influence, innovation, engagement, and change: Cultural savvy persuades, diversifies ideas, boosts morale, and eases transitions.

Conclusion

Cross-cultural leadership transforms challenges into triumphs, creating vibrant teams where diversity drives excellence. Guided by Darwin's adaptability and Romans' renewal, middle leaders who embrace this path unlock boundless potential.

You possess the resilience to navigate sensitivities, the wisdom to foster inclusion, and the vision to inspire unity. Step forward with confidence, your leadership will not only bridge cultures but also elevate all, forging a legacy of harmony and innovation. The world needs your transformative influence now more than ever.

"Whenever you see a successful business, someone once made a courageous decision."

— Peter F. Drucker.

"If any of you lacks wisdom, you should ask God, who gives generously to all without finding fault."

— James 1:5

Chapter 12:
Measuring Your Impact as a Middle Leader

Chapter 11 equipped middle leaders to navigate cultural diversity with adaptive wisdom, drawing from Darwin's responsiveness and Romans' call to mental renewal, harmonizing secular insight with biblical truth to foster inclusive teams.

Yet, true transformation requires not just embracing change but courageously measuring its fruits, as Peter Drucker observed in successful ventures, and **James 1:5** invites divine wisdom for discernment. Chapter 12, "Measuring Your Impact as a Middle Leader," provides the compass for this journey, enabling leaders to track influence, refine actions, and steward their roles faithfully.

Introduction

Middle leaders bridge vision and reality, but without assessment, efforts drift aimlessly. Measuring impact reveals effectiveness in influence, team dynamics, and alignment, fueling growth and informed decisions.

This practice celebrates successes, pinpoints gaps, and builds credibility. Biblical stewardship in **Luke 16:10** and Proverbs **27:23–24** urges diligence in monitoring responsibilities, ensuring faithful service.

The Principle: "If You Don't Measure and Track It, You Can't Manage It"

This maxim, rooted in management wisdom from Peter Drucker, underscores that untracked elements evade control. In leadership, intangible influences like morale or innovation slip away without metrics, leading to assumptions over insights.

Measurement transforms reactivity into proactivity: Quantify team output to spot trends, track feedback to gauge trust. Without it, courageous decisions lack direction; with it, leaders manage spheres effectively, amplifying impact and honoring **James 1:5**'s call for wisdom through evident discernment.

Understanding Your Sphere of Influence

Define domains:

- Team Performance: Goal attainment and productivity.
- Processes: Efficiency gains.
- Culture and Morale: Engagement levels.
- Innovation: Idea generation.

Example: An Amazon fulfillment manager focuses on accuracy and safety, tracking within her control.

Key Metrics for Measuring Impact

1. KPIs for Influence

- Productivity: Output quality.
- Engagement: Initiative rates.
- Retention: Turnover reductions.
- Improvements: Error drops.

Align with org goals; e.g., customer metrics if prioritized.

2. Collecting Feedback

- Upward: Team views on support.
- Peer: Cross-team influence.
- Self: Personal reflections.

Exercise: Monthly 1:1s for insights.

3. Continuous Improvement Metrics

Track reductions in issues, adoption rates, and skill growth.

Biblical Tie: Luke 16:10, small fidelities build trust.

Designing a Leadership Impact Tracker

Components:

- Period: Weekly reviews.
- Area: Specific responsibilities.

- Metric: Quantifiable data.
- Feedback: Qualitative notes.
- Actions: Interventions.
- Outcomes: Results.
- Reflection: Lessons.

Exercise: Build in Excel; review quarterly.

Real-Life Example: Amazon Middle Managers

They monitor fulfillment speeds, feedback on communication, retention trends, driving coaching and processes, enhancing credibility sans broad authority.

Combining Quantitative and Qualitative Measures

Balance metrics (e.g., completion rates) with sentiment (morale feedback). Example: High output but low recognition signals adjustments.

Research Insights

Feedback cultures boost engagement; monitoring aids adjustments (London & Smither, 2002).

Steps for Measuring Leadership Impact

- Define priorities.
- Select metrics.
- Gather data consistently.
- Seek multi-source feedback.
- Reflect and adjust.
- Document progress.
- Celebrate wins.

Biblical Principles

- Luke 16:10: Small trusts yield much.
- Proverbs 27:23–24: Know your flocks' state.
- Colossians 3:23: Heartfelt work for God.

Weekly Action Plan for Measurement

Week 1: Define Spheres

- Map influence areas; select 3 KPIs.
- Reflection: Align with wisdom-seeking prayer.

Week 2: Gather Baseline Data

- Collect initial metrics and feedback.
- Reflection: Gaps revealed?

Week 3: Implement Tracker

- Log data; note actions.
- Reflection: Early insights?

Week 4: Review and Adjust

- Analyze trends; celebrate one win.
- Reflection: Courageous decisions needed?

Ongoing: Monthly feedback loops, quarterly reviews—track with Drucker's courage.

Overcoming Common Measurement Challenges

- Overload: Focus on 5-7 keys.
- Bias: Use anonymous surveys.
- Resistance: Frame as a growth tool.
- Inconsistency: Automate dashboards.

Integrating Measurement with Prior Skills, Case Study, and Long-Term Benefits

Imagine yourself as Alex, a middle manager in a bustling tech firm, where the threads of emotional intelligence, technological savvy, and cross-cultural awareness weave into your daily fabric. Drawing from earlier chapters, you know that EI isn't just a theory; it's the empathetic lens through which you interpret feedback during measurement.

As you roll out your Leadership Impact Tracker, you infuse it with EI by approaching team surveys not as cold data points, but as opportunities to validate feelings and build deeper connections. "How did that project make you feel supported?" you ask in check-ins, turning numbers on engagement scores into narratives of trust and growth.

Technology becomes your ally in this integration, transforming raw data into actionable stories. Using analytics tools like Tableau or Google Data Studio, echoing Chapter 11's digital empowerment, you can dashboard bug rates and collaboration metrics, spotting patterns that EI alone might miss. In cross-cultural teams from Chapter 12, you track diversity metrics: How often do voices from Asian or Latin American colleagues appear in idea logs? This holistic stewardship ensures measurement isn't siloed but a unifying force, adapting to global nuances while leveraging tech for inclusive insights.

Now, picture Alex's real-world turnaround. Facing high turnover and stagnant innovation, he began tracking bug rates alongside engagement surveys. With EI-guided mentoring sessions tailored to cultural preferences, directive for some, collaborative for others, he addressed root causes. Tech tools visualized progress, revealing a **25%** drop in defects and turnover, while innovation spiked through diverse idea submissions. Peers noticed; executives promoted him, seeing data-backed courage.

This integration yields long-term treasures: Resilience blooms as tracked trends weather storms, promotions follow evidenced impact, and accountability deepens, compounding courageous decisions into legacies. Like a ship captain logging winds and stars, you navigate with prior skills as sails, measurement as rudder—arriving not by chance, but charted excellence.

Conclusion

Measuring impact elevates middle leadership from intuition to intentionality, guiding courageous choices with wisdom's light. As a vigilant gardener tracks soil, water, and growth—pruning weaknesses, nourishing strengths, reaping abundant harvests—so must you monitor your leadership orchard, yielding fruits of trust, performance, and legacy. Embrace this discipline: Your measured steps today cultivate thriving tomorrows, stewarding gifts for eternal impact.

"The true measure of leadership is influence - nothing more, nothing less."

— John C. Maxwell.

"Whoever wants to become great among you must be your servant."

— Matthew 20:26

Chapter 13:
Signs of an Effective Middle Leader

Chapter 12 armed middle leaders with the discipline of measurement, turning intangible influence into tangible evidence of growth and stewardship, guided by Drucker's courage and James's wisdom. Yet, beyond metrics lies the lived reality of impact, the subtle signs that your leadership is resonating, even without fanfare. Chapter 13, "Signs of an Effective Middle Leader," illuminates these markers, helping you recognize and amplify your quiet power to shape teams and outcomes.

The Subtle Power of Influence

Influence in the middle often whispers before it commands. Picture a high-stakes project meeting derailing into arguments over deadlines. The formal boss steps out, and instinctively, eyes turn to you. With a timely word, a shared vision reminder, and a quick task breakdown, calm is restored. No decree issued, no title invoked, yet followership emerges. This is middle leadership: quiet authority earned through presence and action.

It manifests in everyday moments, a colleague confiding challenges, a team adopting your suggested process, or conflicts being resolved because you mediated fairly. These aren't accidents; they're evidence of cultivated trust. Recognizing them affirms your role, fueling further growth.

1. People Seek Your Input

When advice flows your way unprompted, influence is at work. It's not about expertise alone but reliability—colleagues value your empathetic ear and ego-free insights.

In workplaces, this bypasses hierarchies: A junior analyst shares ideas with you first, knowing you'll champion them. In communities, neighbors consult you on disputes for your fair perspective.

Proverbs 11:14 highlights safety in counselors; becoming that go-to signals trust-built leadership. Nurture it by listening actively, responding thoughtfully.

Reflection: Track how often input requests arise weekly—what patterns emerge?

2. You Bridge the Gap Between Vision and Reality

Effective middle leaders demystify strategy, turning abstracts into actionable. Senior visions inspire but overwhelm without translation; you provide the roadmap.

Story: In a healthcare nonprofit, executives dreamed of expanded services. Staff froze until a mid-level coordinator mapped 90-day phases, assigned roles, and tied them to daily tasks. Adoption soared, impact followed.

Jesus exemplified this in parables, eternal truths in relatable tales of sowers and prodigal sons. Similarly, break down goals: "This quarter's target means two client calls weekly per team member."

Sign: Teams grasp and execute big pictures through your lens.

3. You Empower Others Rather Than Compete With Them

Impact shows in others' elevation. Do direct reports innovate freely? Peers collaborate without rivalry?

Empowerment shares spotlights: Delegate stretch projects, credit ideas publicly. A sales supervisor who trains reps to lead meetings sees promotions ripple, not threats, but legacies.

Matthew 20:26 calls greatness servanthood. Measure by thriving around you: Retention high? Skills blooming?

Example: A school department head empowered teachers with curriculum input; test scores rose, morale soared, and attrition dropped.

4. You Lead With Consistency and Integrity

Steadiness anchors chaos. Consistency in values, delivering promises, and admitting errors builds dependability.

During crises, like budget cuts, your calm ethics guide: Transparent communications prevent rumors.

Psalm 15 praises oath-keepers. Colleagues predict your reactions, trusting the bridge you provide.

Narrative: In a tech startup crunch, a mid-manager upheld ethics amid shortcuts, retaining talent and respect, leading to sustainable success.

5. You're Making Impact Without Demanding the Spotlight

True influence operates backstage. Projects succeed via your connections, and cultures shift from your quiet advocacy.

Paul, in 1 Corinthians 3:7, notes that planters and waterers yield to God's growth, focus on sowing.

Sign: Anonymous wins attribute to "the team's effort," yet you orchestrated.

Additional Signs of Effectiveness

- Conflicts Resolve Constructively Around You: You facilitate win-wins, drawing from EI to de-escalate.

- Innovation Sparks in Your Presence: Ideas flow freely, as psychological safety reigns.

- Feedback Loops Strengthen: Teams give and receive input openly, fostering growth.

- Adaptability in Change: You guide through shifts, measuring responses per prior chapters.

- Personal Growth Evident: Your self-leadership (Chapter 9) models humility, inspiring emulation.

Biblical and Practical Integration

James 3:17 describes wisdom pure, peaceable, mirroring these signs. Drucker's courageous decisions align with faithful steps.

Exercise: Journal weekly signs observed; seek peer validation.

Research Insights

Gallup finds that trusted middle managers boost engagement **20%**; Zenger Folkman studies link empowerment to top-quartile performance.

Weekly Action Plan to Cultivate Signs

Week 1: Seek Input—Invite advice requests explicitly.

Week 2: Bridge Visions—Translate one strategy session.

Week 3: Empower Actively—Delegate a key task.

Week 4: Demonstrate Consistency—Follow through publicly.

Ongoing: Track subtle impacts, reflect biblically.

Overcoming Obstacles to Recognition

Doubt creeps: "Am I really leading?" Counter with measurement integration (Chapter 13), log instances.

In toxic cultures, signs may subtly emerge; persist in integrity.

Case Studies

- Corporate: A marketing mid-leader's bridging turned vague campaigns into hits, earning voluntary followership.

- Family: An older sibling's empowerment resolved household dynamics, modeling Matthew's servanthood.

Conclusion: Building Toward a Roadmap

These signs affirm your middle leadership's potency, subtle yet seismic, influencing without insignia. As roots nourish trees unseen yet essential, your efforts sustain organizational life. Recognizing them propels you forward; now, synthesize into action.

"Plans are nothing; planning is everything."
— Dwight D. Eisenhower

"Commit to the Lord whatever you do, and he will establish your plans."
— Proverbs 16:3

Chapter 14:
Your Middle Leadership Roadmap

Chapter 13 provided tools to measure impact, transforming assumptions into evidence through disciplined tracking and reflection. Now, synthesize these insights into a cohesive strategy. Chapter 14, "Your Middle Leadership Roadmap," offers a practical framework to align purpose, actions, and influence for sustained excellence.

This chapter offers the roadmap, weaving self-leadership, tech, culture, and measurement into a blueprint for enduring success. Step boldly, for your influence shapes eternities.

Introduction

Middle leaders bridge vision and execution without ultimate authority, making intentionality essential. A roadmap structures actions, aligns with goals, and fosters growth amid challenges.

Eisenhower's quote emphasizes planning's primacy; **Proverbs 16:3** anchors it in faith. Seek wisdom (**James 1:5**) to balance demands ethically.

This chapter details steps, exercises, templates, and biblical integration for a dynamic plan.

Step 1: Clarify Your Leadership Purpose

Define why you lead to guide decisions.

Questions: What impact do you seek? How do values align with mission?

Exercise: Craft a statement: "I lead to empower teams with empathy, driving innovation ethically."

Biblical: Psalm 37:5—commit ways to God for action.

Reflection: What motivates you daily? Which strengths leverage?

Step 2: Map Your Sphere of Influence

Identify impact areas: teams, peers, processes, culture.

Exercise: Concentric circles diagram—center: self; inner: direct reports; outer: organization.

Example: Starbucks' Schultz mapped to reinforce servant culture.

Narrative: A hospital coordinator mapped nursing shifts, optimizing morale and efficiency.

Step 3: Set Clear, Achievable Goals

Use the SMART framework for relevance.

Tip: 90-day cycles build momentum.

Example: Enhance collaboration via bi-weekly forums; measure the rise in participation.

Questions: Aligned? Resourced?

Biblical: Proverbs 21:5—diligent plans lead to abundance.

Step 4: Develop Action Plans

Translate goals into steps.

Template Table:

Goal	Action Steps	Resources Needed	Timeline	Success Metrics
Improve communication	Implement check-ins; train on tools	Platforms like Teams; time allocation	Weeks 1-4 setup; ongoing	Feedback scores up 20%; fewer misunderstandings
Develop talent	Pair mentors; track progress	Internal experts; scheduling app	Monthly sessions	Promotions internal +15%
Optimize processes	Audit workflows; pilot changes	Data tools; team input	Quarter 1	Efficiency gain 10%; error reduction

Guidance: Assign owners, set checkpoints, adapt.

Example: Tech manager's mentorship plan: Identify potentials (Week 1), match pairs (Week 2), monitor (ongoing)—skill gaps closed.

Step 5: Reflection and Self-Assessment

Weekly journaling tracks growth.

Questions: Impacts? Improvements needed?

Exercise: Log decisions, outcomes; review monthly.

Story: The Engineer reflected on failed pitches, adjusted EI approaches, and secured funding.

Biblical: Lamentations 3:40—examine ways.

Step 6: Engage in Mentorship and Coaching

Sharpen others mutually.

Practices: Guide without authority; peer exchanges; talent spotting.

Biblical: 2 Timothy 2:2—entrust to reliable; Proverbs 27:17—iron sharpens.

Exercise: Team roadmap: Milestones like skill workshops; track stories.

Example: Nonprofit director coached cross-culturally, boosting retention.

Step 7: Integrate Tools and Technology

Enhance efficiency.

Applications: Slack for comms; Tableau for metrics; LinkedIn for branding.

Questions: Supports goals? Simplifies?

Example: Dropbox aligned via Asana, influencing remotely.

Integration: Link to measurement (Chapter 13)—dashboards auto-track.

Step 8: Align with Organizational Vision and Values

Bridge strategy daily.

Steps: Review initiatives; translate objectives; communicate purpose.

Biblical: James 1:5—ask for wisdom for alignment.

Narrative: Finance mid-leader tied audits to ethics, earning trust amid scandals.

Step 9: Track Progress and Adjust

Living document reviews.

Methods: Weekly action checks; quarterly reassessments.

Exercise: Adjustment log—what shifted, why?

Example: Retail manager pivoted goals post-market change, saving campaigns.

Step 10: Model Integrity and Servant Leadership

Core to influence.

Actions: Ethical decisions; own outcomes; celebrate the team.

Biblical: Matthew 20:26—servant greatness.

Example: Schultz's 90-day plans balanced profits, people, and legacy endured.

Expanded Exercises and Templates

Purpose Worksheet: Values list; align to statement.

Influence Map Template: Circles with stakeholders, opportunities.

Goal Setting Sheet: SMART breakdown per quarter.

Journal Prompts: Weekly: Wins/challenges; Monthly: Biblical applications.

Mentorship Tracker:

Mentee	Goals	Sessions	Progress Notes	Feedback
John	Presentation skills	Bi-weekly	Improved confidence	Positive peer reviews

Tech Audit: Tools list; usage effectiveness; gaps.

Weekly/Quarterly Action Plan

Week 1-4: Purpose/sphere mapping.

Month 2: Goals/actions draft.

Quarter End: Full review, adjust.

Ongoing: Daily integrity checks; prayerful commitments.

Research Insights

Harvard: Planned leaders **30%** more effective; Gallup: Aligned roadmaps boost engagement **21%**.

Case Studies

- Healthcare: Nurse supervisor road-mapped shifts, reduced burnout by **40%**.

- Tech: PM integrated tools/mentoring, project delivery 25% faster.

- Education: Principal-aligned vision, test scores up, culture transformed.

Challenges and Solutions

Challenge: Resistance—Solution: Involve the team in planning.

Overload: Prioritize 3 goals max.

Biblical Encouragement: Proverbs 16:9—man plans, God directs.

Humility Under Christ: Leading from the Middle in God's Order

All lead from the middle under Christ (Colossians 1:18). CEOs are accountable upward; entry-level employees influence peers. Shifts focus: Stewardship, not empire-building. Empowers all roles with Kingdom purpose.

Reflection: How does Christ's headship humble/embolden your roadmap?

Closing Thoughts

This roadmap, purpose-driven, actionable, and reflective, equips influential middle leadership. Commit plans prayerfully; seek wisdom liberally.

Eisenhower valued the planning process; Scripture establishes divine alignment. Embrace: Your intentional path influences profoundly, stewarding gifts eternally.

"Train up a child in the way he should go; even when he is old, he will not depart from it."
— Proverbs 22:6 (Biblical)

"The family is the first essential cell of human society."
— Pope John Paul II (Professional/Thought Leader)

Chapter 15:
Leading Up with Humility and Strength

I'll never forget the day a mentor pulled me aside after a meeting. He could tell I was frustrated. The project we'd been working on was moving too slowly. Our leader had made another decision that didn't make sense, and I was doing everything in my power not to show it on my face.

He looked at me and said quietly, "Richard, God's not testing your ability right now, He's testing your attitude."

I stood there stunned. He continued, "Anyone can lead when they're in charge. But only mature leaders can lead when they're not."

That conversation stuck with me. It reframed everything I understood about influence, authority, and humility. I began to see that leadership wasn't about position; it was about posture.

The Refining Ground

There will come a time in every leader's life when their skills outgrow their surroundings. You may be more experienced than the person you report to. You may think faster, see clearer, or lead stronger. You may even feel like you're carrying more weight than your title reflects.

That's not a sign of failure; it's a season of formation.

The Bible is filled with examples of overqualified leaders serving under imperfect ones. Joseph managed households and prisons before managing nations. David had the heart of a king long before he had the crown. Even Jesus spent years in obscurity as a carpenter, quietly obedient, before stepping into public ministry.

God often hides greatness in humility. The middle is where He shapes your heart before He reveals your capacity.

Proverbs 3:5–6 (NIV): *"Trust in the Lord with all your heart and lean not on your own understanding; in all your ways submit to Him, and He will make your paths straight."*

It's easy to submit when you agree. It's faith when you submit and don't understand.

Learning to Lead Up

Leading from the middle means learning how to lead up—and that takes a special kind of maturity.

When you're under leadership that frustrates you, you have two choices: you can lead with frustration, or you can lead with faith. Frustration will make you critical. Faith will make you creative.

I began to change my approach. Instead of pointing out flaws, I started asking better questions. Instead of pushing for my way, I focused on helping my leader succeed in their way.

The shift was subtle but powerful. My influence grew, not because I demanded it, but because I earned it through consistency and humility.

Leading up is not about proving you're smarter; it's about proving you're steady. It's not about showing your superiority; it's about showing your support.

Philippians 2:3–4 (ESV): *"Do nothing from selfish ambition or conceit, but in humility count others more significant than yourselves."*

Humility doesn't suppress your ability, it strengthens your credibility.

The Heart Work

There were moments when pride whispered in my ear: *If I were in charge, we'd already be there by now.*

It's in those moments that God often works the deepest. He doesn't rebuke your ability—He refines your motives.

One day during prayer, I sensed God saying, *"If you can't serve leadership you disagree with, you're not ready to be a leader others depend on."*

That truth hit hard. Leadership isn't just about vision; it's about submission. If you can't handle being under authority, you're not ready to carry it.

So I shifted again. I stopped focusing on the limitations of my leader and started focusing on my responsibility to the mission. I could still bring ideas, excellence, and energy, but I had to do it with respect and restraint.

That's when peace entered the tension. I learned that the middle isn't just a job position, it's a heart position.

God's Timing and Organizational Wisdom

In organizational leadership, success is often measured by visibility. The higher you climb, the more people assume you're winning. But in God's Kingdom, the opposite is true. The deeper you serve, the more He prepares you for what's ahead.

Psalm 75:6–7 (NKJV): *"For exaltation comes neither from the east nor from the west nor from the south. But God is the Judge: He puts down one, and exalts another."*

Your next opportunity won't come from who notices you, it will come from who sent you.

When David served under Saul, he had every right to take matters into his own hands. He was anointed, capable, and ready. But David refused to take a shortcut to the throne. He honored Saul's position even when Saul dishonored him.

That's not weakness, that's wisdom. The same God who anointed David was also testing him to see if he could lead with integrity when no one was watching.

Integrity in the Middle

Integrity is the invisible currency of leadership. It's not about being perfect, it's about being trustworthy.

There were times when I disagreed deeply with the direction we were going. I could have rallied others to my side or quietly sabotaged the plan, but I knew that wasn't leadership; it was rebellion dressed in frustration.

Instead, I chose to honor publicly and question privately. I protected my leader's credibility even when I felt unseen. And over time, that quiet faithfulness opened more doors than ambition ever could.

When people saw that I wasn't trying to climb over others, they began to trust me to lead among them.

The Middle as a Making Place

The middle is not punishment, it's preparation.

It's where God works out impatience, softens pride, and strengthens endurance. It's where you learn how to influence without a title and lead without applause. It's where your character is formed to match your calling.

When you finally step into greater leadership, you'll realize that the humility you built in the middle is the strength that sustains you at the top.

Galatians 6:9 (NIV): *"Let us not become weary in doing good, for at the proper time we will reap a harvest if we do not give up."*

If you find yourself today under a leader you could outperform, don't lose heart. You're not being overlooked—you're being over-prepared. God is shaping you for a stage you haven't stepped onto yet.

Lead with humility. Serve with strength. Influence with integrity. And when your time comes, you won't have to reach for the next level; God will lift you to it.

Leadership Insight Sidebar

Leading Up with Humility and Strength

- Serve the mission, not your ego. Your influence grows when you focus on outcomes, not recognition.

- Honor authority, even when imperfect. Respect doesn't require agreement; it requires integrity.

- Lead quietly, impact powerfully. Excellence under observation often speaks louder than authority ever could.

- Stay faithful in the middle. Seasons of preparation are often longer than we expect, but God's timing is perfect.

- Humility is strength. Leading with restraint, empathy, and patience builds credibility and character that lasts.

Chapter 16:
Leading from the Middle at Home

Introduction

Imagine a bustling household on a typical evening: Dinner simmers on the stove, kids argue over homework, and a spouse juggles calls from work. In this chaos, leadership isn't about who holds the parental title; it's about who steps in to listen, guide, and unite. Home is your original leadership arena, where influence is raw, relational, and eternal. Here, we've all led from the middle long before boardrooms: As kids negotiating bedtime, as parents balancing authority with empathy, as siblings forging alliances.

This chapter exhorts you gently: Bring workplace principles home, for family's stakes are higher, hearts, not just metrics. Empathetically, I know life's demands pull you thin; yet, incorporating these builds resilience, joy, and faith. Your efforts here echo eternally, shaping generations with love's quiet power.

Leading from the Middle: A Family Definition

In families, no one reigns supreme; it's a circle of influence. Parents guide amid cultural pressures; children shape norms through actions; siblings negotiate daily. Leading from the middle means empowering each member's voice: Parents model listening over dictating, kids initiate kindness, and extended family offers wisdom.

Narrate this: A father, stressed from work, chooses vulnerability, "Today was tough; how was yours?" inviting shares, diffusing tensions. A child, seeing this, mirrors by helping a sibling, rippling respect. Empathetically, if hierarchies dominate your home, start small; exhortatively, this shared approach fosters unity, reducing conflicts by **30%** per family studies (American Psychological Association). Biblically, **Deuteronomy 6:6-7** urges teaching diligently in daily life, middle leadership incarnate.

The Ripple Effect of Family Leadership

Every home action sends waves. A harsh word lingers like storm clouds; encouragement, sunlight's warmth. Exhorting you: Recognize your pebbles' power, patience teaches resilience, as a mom pausing mid-argument models grace, her teen later emulating in friendships.

Story: In a blended family, a stepparent's consistent fairness bridged divides; kids thrived, echoing in their empathy. Empathetically, failures happen; forgive yourself. Research shows reflective homes boost child well-being by **25%** (Harvard Family Research). Incorporate principles: Measure ripples via family check-ins, mentor through shared stories, and home becomes harmony's lab.

Parents as Middle Leaders

Parents, you're sandwiched: Above, societal expectations; below, children's needs. Lead middling by filtering influences healthily—curate media, infuse values.

Narrative: A dad, amid financial strain, transparently shares prayers, teaching trust in God; kids learn stewardship. Exhort: Empower over control, delegate choices like meal planning. Tone empathetically: Exhaustion is absolute; **Proverbs 22:6** promises long-term fruits from faithful training.

Children as Leaders-in-the-Middle

Kids lead now, influencing moods, habits. Teach: Your choices matter.

Imagine: A 10-year-old consoles an upset sibling, shifting the home's tone. Exhort families: Affirm this, "That's leadership!" Empathetically, kids falter; guide with grace, building confidence. **1 Timothy 4:12** empowers youth examples.

Siblings as Middle Leaders

Siblings master middle dynamics from rivalry to teamwork.

Story: Middle child mediates fights, fostering peace. Exhort: Coach "team" mindsets, "How help each other shine?" Reduces conflicts, per sibling studies. **Proverbs 27:17** sharpens mutually.

Practical Ways Families Can Practice Leading from the Middle

- Family Meetings: Weekly circles, voices equal. Discuss outings; kids propose, parents guide. Builds ownership.

- Rotating Roles: Lead prayers, chores, and empower all.

- Storytelling Evenings: Share influences; reflects Chapter 14 signs.

- Model Apology/Forgiveness: Parents apologize first, humility ripples.

- Shared Mission: Craft statement: "Love God, respect all." Guides decisions.

- Celebrate Leadership: Note initiatives, "You led beautifully, helping Grandma."

Integrate roadmap (Chapter 14): Purpose sessions, goal family goals like "Weekly service project."

Empathetic tone: Start small amid busyness; exhort: Consistency yields bonded homes.

Biblical Anchors for Family Leadership

- Joshua 24:15: Household service declaration.

- Ephesians 6:4: Gentle instruction.

- 1 Timothy 4:12: Youth examples.

- Proverbs 27:17: Sharpening.

Pope John Paul II's cell of society underscores the family's societal role, leading to strengthening foundations.

Incorporating Principles: Why It Matters

Dear reader, empathetically: Homes fracture under unchecked hierarchies; I've seen exhaustion from "top-down" parenting. Yet, exhorting with hope, these principles heal. Workplace self-discipline (Chapter 9) becomes patient listening; tech (Chapter 11) family apps for coordination; culture (Chapter 12) respects diverse ages.

Story: A family applied meetings, teens shared burdens, parents mentored; bonds deepened, faith grew. Why vital? Shapes character, kids learn empathy, resilience; adults model Christ. Studies: Involved families reduce youth risks **50%** (CDC). Biblically, homes reflect God's family (**Ephesians 3:15**), and middle leadership mirrors servant love.

Exhort: Begin tonight, a shared prayer committing plans (**Proverbs 16:3**). Your influence here outshines careers, nurturing souls for eternity.

Conclusion: Eternal Ripples

Leading from the middle at home transforms ordinary moments into legacies. Empathetically embrace imperfections; exhortatively persist, your waves shape worlds. As pebbles unite into mighty currents, so your family's shared influence flows into society, glorifying the ultimate Head, Christ.

Epilogue:
The Eternal Measure of Middle Leadership

Dear reader, as we reach the culmination of this journey through the art of leading from the middle, pause and reflect: You stand not at the pinnacle of power nor the base of obscurity, but in the vital heart of influence, where true transformation pulses. Throughout these pages, we've unearthed the professional bedrock of trust-building, political navigation, change-driving, emotional mastery, coaching excellence, technological leverage, cultural bridging, impact measurement, subtle effectiveness, and strategic roadmapping. Woven inseparably are the timeless biblical threads: Jonathan's sacrificial loyalty, David's resilient faith, Nehemiah's unified rebuilding, Proverbs' sharpened wisdom, Matthew's servant greatness, Romans' renewed mind, James' generous wisdom, and Colossians' Christ-centered order.

And extending this tapestry to the hearth, we've seen how these principles illuminate family life, parents as empathetic bridges, children as emerging influencers, siblings as collaborative sharpeners, rippling Kingdom values into generations.

Now, exhorting you with fervent urgency: Embrace this calling! In the boardroom's tensions or the dinner table's chaos, lead not for acclaim but for eternal impact. Professionally, measure your steps with Drucker's courage, wielding EI's empathy and tech's precision to forge inclusive cultures amid volatility. Remember, untracked influence fades, but diligent stewardship multiplies. Biblically, commit your plans to the Lord as Proverbs urges, modeling Christ's servanthood to lift others, for as iron sharpens iron, your faithfulness in the middle echoes heaven's design.

At home, tenderly yet boldly incorporate these, listen as families circle in meetings, empower through rotating roles, celebrate ripples of kindness for the family is society's cell, and your middle leadership there shapes souls far beyond careers.

Vital truth: This isn't optional; it's your divine commission. In a world craving authenticity amid division, your integrated life, professional poise, biblical anchor, and familial grace become the beacon. Rise, then! Step boldly into the middle, where influence blooms unseen yet unstoppably.

Commit today: Lead with integrity's consistency, wisdom's discernment, and love's extravagance. The Kingdom advances through such faithful middles, yours included. Go forth, measure your legacy in lives transformed, and watch God establish your path eternally.

www.ingramcontent.com/pod-product-compliance
Lightning Source LLC
Chambersburg PA
CBHW040901210326
41597CB00029B/4922